Do You Know that You Have Black Friends?

SUNY series in African American Studies

Marion Orr, Pearl Dowe, and Ravi K. Perry, editors

Do You Know that You Have Black Friends?

A Reeducation on Race for White Americans by Black Americans

Timothy Elijah Lewis

SUNY
PRESS

Published by State University of New York Press, Albany

Printed in the United States of America

EU GPSR Authorised Representative:
Logos Europe, 9 rue Nicolas Poussin, 17000, La Rochelle, France
contact@logoseurope.eu

For information, contact State University of New York Press, Albany, NY
www.sunypress.edu

Library of Congress Cataloging-in-Publication Data

Names: Lewis, Timothy Elijah, 1985- author
Title: Do you know that you have Black friends? : a reeducation on race for white Americans by Black Americans / Timothy Elijah Lewis.
Description: Albany : State University of New York Press, 2026. | Series: SUNY series in African Aamerican studies | Includes bibliographical references and index.
Identifiers: LCCN 2026007539 | ISBN 9798855809329 hardcover | ISBN 9798855809343 pdf | ISBN 9798855809350 ebook | ISBN 9798855809336 paperback
Subjects: LCSH: African Americans—Social conditions | African Americans—Race identity | Race—Social aspects—United States | United States—Race relations
Classification: LCC E185.86 .L4936 2026
LC record available at https://lccn.loc.gov/2026007539

To my late father, Mr. Perry Lewis II, and to every Black person who endured the dehumanization embedded in the social construct of race in America yet managed to smile and laugh big . . . "GREAT DAY!"

Contents

Illustrations

Forethought

When W. E. B. Du Bois wrote *The Souls of Black Folk*, he diagnosed a sick US society by affirming that "the problem of the Twentieth Century [was] the problem of the color line." The color line was not simply the recognition that Black and White people occupy different social categories. Rather it meant that because of visible differences, they have been assigned fundamentally different life experiences. The color line did not simply categorize; it sentenced. Those who were Black were sentenced to lives structured by pervasive oppression and perpetual disadvantage, while those who were White were ordained to lives of uninhibited liberty, privilege, and unearned advantages. More than one hundred years later, the color line still exists.

But why does the persistence of this "problem" function as a cancer for both the White and Black Americans? It is a problem for the White Americans because the Black spirit is one of resilience and triumph — one that constantly bucks the system's design in pursuit of true liberation. Black people have always challenged inequity and injustice and will continue to do so, even when denied the recourses necessary to achieve their aspirations. And the acts of Black resilience serve as damning mirrors, reflecting back to White people the grotesque failure of a "divinely appointed" democracy that was, in truth, founded on the theology of exclusion.

On the other hand, this system of White advantage remains a problem for Black Americans, because White people will claim an aspiration for racial equity while refusing to confront the uncomfortable truths of racial oppression. This means that Black people will wait for the day that White actions match voiced aspirations, while knowing that such a day will likely not arrive within their lifetime.

We are now more than a century removed from Du Bois's publishing of *The Souls of Black Folk*, and I can say emphatically that he was shortsighted. The color line was not a temporary hurdle of the twentieth century; it is the defining architecture of the American soul. Race — and the inherent inequality it perpetuates — remains the American problem, indefinitely!

Acknowledgments

Dr. Sherice J. Nelson
Nicole Franklin
Youthen Joseph
Karyn Thomas
Dr. Emmitt Riley
Dr. Sharon Austin
The National Conference of Black Political Scientists (NCOBPS)
Southern Illinois University Edwardsville
Harris–Stowe State University
The Church of Christ

Chapter 1

"I Have Black Friends"

An Illegitimate Defense of White Racism

"You get them niggers!" Those were the words Tabitha Duncan chose to use, not in 1958, but in a 2018 viral video where the intoxicated White waitress and enlistee in the Air Force Reserve gleefully joined in a racist dialogue about "nigger hunting." The video clip, or the fifteen seconds that went viral, shows Duncan sitting on the roof of a truck with a bottle of beer in her hand while she and her friends slowly drive down a gravel road at night, all the while repeating *nigger* into the smartphone's camera recorder. With honest candor, the derogatory and contemptuous diction in the video may not have been necessarily shocking to most Black Americans. After all, a quick investigation of the word would show that racism against Black people has seldom been employed without the recitation of the word *nigger*.

The word, as a derogatory insult, has been used since the 1700s to impose contempt on Blacks as an inferior race. Hosea Easton (1837) discusses the origins of the word *nigge*r in the *Treatise on the Intellectual Character and Civil and Political Condition of the Colored People of the United States, and the Prejudice Exercised Towards Them*. Easton explains how the word *nigger* came from a deplorable child-rearing strategy in which White parents would reprimand children for undesirable behavior by comparing their behavior to that of the "nigger." It was common for White parents to threaten their children with coexistence with Black slaves, telling their children that unless they behaved well, they would be carried off by "the old nigger." It was in this period of slavery, decades before the US Civil War, that the term *nigger* served as the primary reference to Black people — a way of referring "derogatorily, contemptuously, and often menacingly to Blacks" (Kennedy, 1999, 87). So, for more than two centuries, Black Americans have heard White people refer to them by the demoralizing term that Tabitha Duncan repeated in her drunken stupor.

However, it was Duncan's rebuttal to the online backlash that flustered me and may have raised an eyebrow of concern from many Black people. After the racist video went viral on social media platforms like Snapchat and garnered hundreds of thousands of views across social media outlets, Duncan attempted to denounce valid accusations of racism and defend herself by saying, "I have Black friends, I have Black people in my family, I didn't mean it" (Murphy, 2018, para. 8). Again, Duncan's drunk tirade of racism is not novel to the lived Black experience, but the supposed defense "I have Black friends," or the family defense — "I have Black people in my family," seem all too often to be the defense of White Americans when accused of racism. It appears to be the default, almost scripted, alibi for White people to affirm in moments where obvious anti-Black racism cannot be denied, and the examples are endless.

In early 2019, when a racist yearbook image of Virginia Governor Ralph Northam emerged with one person in blackface and another in a Ku Klux Klan costume, to which Northam confirms being one of the people, he used the defense until national outrage forced a more compelling apology. At a CNN news conference, Northam stated, "I was in public school during desegregation. I have a lot of African American friends that I went to school with, played ball with. And I suspect I've had as much exposure to people of color as anybody." If Governor Northam really had as many Black friends as he stated, wouldn't he have known that either costume — Blackface or Klansman — were offensive, inappropriate, and could trigger trauma in those Black friends? However, Duncan and Northam are not unique examples. Referring to Black proximity is the typical customary response for White and White-identifying people when public actions are racist or even racially ignorant. In the 2024 Republican Primary season, former US Ambassador to the United Nations Nikki Haley failed to accurately affirm that slavery was the cause of the Civil War. As damage control Haley, who once identified as White on a voter registration card (doing what *Politico* calls a "complicated racial dance"), scurried to the script (Martinez and Booker, 2024). She told MSNBC and CNN that she "had Black friends growing up" (Lim, 2024, para. 4). But, again, if she had Black friends, as she affirmed, wouldn't she have readily known that the fundamental issue of the Civil War was a contention over slavery?

I affirm that the affirmation of having "Black friends" is so ingrained in White culture that White people will use the defense even when they are not indicted of racism but as a defense of other White people. An example is Governor Northam's childhood friend, Harry Mears, who came to his defense, repeating the affirmation of Black friends. He told *The New York Times*, "[Northam] is the last person on earth that would be racist [because] … we have just as many Black friends together as we do White friends." Likely a better-known political example occurred during the 2019 congressional hearing of Michael Cohen before the House of Representatives Oversight Committee. During that hearing, Republican Congressman Mark Meadows used Lynne Patton, an African American woman, as a counternarrative to Cohen's testimony, which exposed the racist words and actions of President Donald Trump. In this instance, Representative Meadows was using Black association as a defense of someone else, President Trump. Congresswoman Rashida Tlaib responded to Meadows by saying, "Just because someone has a person of color — a Black person — working for them does not mean they aren't racist" (NBC News, 2019). Tlaib's assertion fell short, as Congressman Meadows doubled down by informing of his own familial proximity to Black people, even pleading that Representative Elijah Cummings, a Black American and Chair of the Committee, to explain to Tlaib that he had "nieces and nephews … of color."

These instances show a normative belief in White culture — verbalizing proximity to someone racialized as Black, such as Black friends or family, should vindicate a White person from words and actions that are clearly racist. If the charges were racism or even simple racial ignorance, then Black proximity is the defense's evidence that should emphatically render a "not guilty" verdict. But is having Black friends a legitimate defense? Does being close to people racialized as Black absolve one, specifically White people, from being racist?

An Illegitimate Defense

Again, having "Black friends" or being in proximity to Black people has become the default alibi to exonerate White racism, and the abundance of examples informs those who are not White that the presumption is cultural. It is customary that relational proximity to a Black person discredits the accusations that their thoughts, words, or behaviors are substantively racist. The cultural assumption is based on the incorrect perception that racism necessitates the avoidance of Black people, particularly avoiding relationships based on love, fidelity, and loyalty, such as those characterizing friendships and family. It informs quite conspicuously of White thinking — that if a White person voluntarily chooses close intimate proximity to persons racialized as Black, they cannot be racist. The claim, however, is illegitimate because it is rooted in two falsehoods.

First, the theory on which the claim is based is itself false, as it assumes that individual racism is antagonistic to self-selected Black interactions. However, US history, starting with this country's inception, shows us that Black proximity is no defense against interpersonal racism. The "Founding Fathers" often had sexual interactions with slaves, which ranged from the common raping of slaves to complicated relationships with the obvious imbalanced master-slave power dynamic. Most notable of these was Thomas Jefferson's relationship with Sally Hemings, a young Black female slave owned by Jefferson. Jefferson publicly avowed his love for Hemings, even temporarily relocating to France, where Hemings would be free, and the power dynamics in Jefferson's favor would have somewhat diminished. However, Jefferson's self-proclaimed love for Hemings did not prevent the enslavement of 600 Black people at his plantation at Monticello, some of those slaves being his own biracial children that he had fathered with Hemings (CBS News, 2012). Jefferson, often seen as one of the most benevolent of the "Founding Fathers," had a relationship with Sally Hemings that has been proven by DNA testing, yet his own children were enslaved under the dehumanizing system of chattel slavery. If the premise of having Black family members excused racism, then Jefferson, like John Adams and Thomas Paine, would not have participated in the system of slavery (Austin, 2020).

Figure 1.1. Alice Jones. *Source*: *The Broad Ax*, December 12, 1925. Library of Congress. Public domain.

But it is not necessary to reach back to the horrors of slavery for an example that proves Black proximity does not negate anti-Black racism. An example outside the system of chattel slavery is that of Leonard Rhinelander. In 1924 Leonard Rhinelander married a biracial woman who identified as Black, Alice Jones. And though Rhineland knew Jones was Black over their three-year courtship, he thought she could pass as White because of her light pigmentation. However, when the socialites of New York, particularly his family, discovered that Jones, who had become Rhineland's wife, was Black, he manifested his racism by attempting to have the marriage annulled, even degrading Alice as a "vamp" that tricked him (Behan, 2007). Alice was forced to the extreme tactic of stripping before an all-White, all-male jury to exonerate herself and her character and win a yearly allowance from Rhinelander, as it was clear she was "colored" (PBS, 2013). Again, if Black proximity was a legitimate defense, then Rhinelander would not have made a public and legal spectacle of his own wife.

Jefferson and Rhinelander are examples among a long record of White people who have proximity to and voluntary interactions with Black people, even romantic relationships, yet are obviously racist. The list includes Strom Thurmond, a vocal segregationist, who filibustered a civil rights bill by speaking for twenty-four hours on the Senate floor. Thurmond was so publicly antagonistic to equal rights for Black Americans that when President Johnson signed the Civil Rights Act, Thurmond switched parties and became a Republican in protest. However, when Thurmond was twenty-two years old, he had a romantic relationship (using those words delicately) with Carrie Butler, his Black fifteen-year-old housemaid, and fathered a biracial daughter, Essie Mae-Washington, whom he hid his entire life (Coleman, 2013). These examples show clearly that having a closeness to Black people, whether by romantic interest, platonic friendship, or family, does not negate one from being racist. It is simply false, and perhaps delusional, to believe that if one voluntarily interacts with a Black person, that individual cannot be racist.

Beyond the Black proximity defense being an outright false belief, the presumption that individual racism negates voluntary Black interactions demonstrates a misunderstanding of race and, by consequence, a misunderstanding of racism. There is no irony that the racial group with the most racial privilege has the greatest misunderstanding of race, or more accurately, how a racial system is inherently discriminatory. The thought that closeness eliminates racism narrowly and ignorantly redefines racism as simple disdain for persons of a different race. That is not true and therein is the second falsehood revealed. It is incorrect to believe that if one has no racial animus or disdain and never performs any discriminatory actions, then that person is not racist. Even if it were possible to successfully exonerate oneself from individual racism, also called interpersonal racism, there are still other behaviors, thoughts, and actions can be substantively racist. Dr. Lee Ann Bell teaches that racism is "a pervasive system of advantage and disadvantage based on the socially-constructed category of race," with multiple types and levels all connected to "sustain systemic benefits for Whites as a group" (Bell et al., 2016, 134).

Dr. Bell's definition informs us of several things about racism that may not be commonly known. First, it informs us that in a racial system, there will be racial categories that experience greater degrees of disadvantage than others. As a matter of fact, Bell teaches that is the intent of racial categories — to assign some societal benefit to some over others, and in the US, those benefits or privileges were allocated to White people. Dr. Richard Middleton (2008) builds on Bell's affirmation that race in the US is a system designed to advantage those racialized as White. Middleton provides some important history of race's construction in the US going back to the 1600s, when biracialism was an offense culturally and legally. Middleton calls it the "rule of hypodescent," where the nuances of mixed-race people were irrelevant, as the construction of race wanted to circumvent any difficulties that would complicate White supremacy (2008, 4). Either you were White or non-White, where "Whiteness was made to be the desired racial status" (Middleton, 2008, 5). Bell and Middleton confirm that race is a hierarchy, and the disadvantages experienced by some groups are simply the system of race acting according to its design.

Additionally, Bell's use of the adjective *pervasive* informs us that in a racial system, racism is everywhere — the unfair enforcement of that racial hierarchy is everywhere, and its evidence is everywhere. This should be educational to any individual seeking to absolve themselves of racism simply because they do not have conscious racial disdain. Because racism is everywhere, one does not have to be conscious of stereotypes, attitudes, behaviors, and words that spark or reinforce racial marginalization. More importantly, racism is more than individually manifested. Racism can be institutional, societal, cultural, and structural.

Finally, and as affirmed by the previous examples, Dr. Bell's definition informs that closeness to Black people is not the abdication from individual racism that White people should pursue. If White people sincerely want to prove themselves as antiracist, then it should be less about proving that their individual acts are not racist through nearness to Black people. The true exonerations from racism will rest with repetitive actions/patterns that challenge the system that is advantageous to some while simultaneously disadvantaging others, particularly Black Americans. This is discussed in the final chapter of the book; however, if racism rests on the advantages and disadvantages that some racial groups are defined by, then systemic correction to diminish or erase those disadvantages is the measuring stick of antiracism.

If someone could conclude that closeness to Black people is an illegitimate defense to racism, as they should, why are there so many examples of White people clinging to the faulty defense? I affirm that the answer is ignorance. The central premise of this book is that there exists a general racial ignorance about race among White populations. This ignorance and the need for learning is evinced in something as simple as how White Americans talk about race. White conversations about race may admit to, if not focus on, the discriminatory treatment and practices endured by non-White persons but never the need for White people to relinquish the benefits of a racialized society if they are even willing to make that admission (Bell et al., 2016). However, it is the presumption of Black racial activists for more than a century that this ignorance can be dispelled through education, or in this sense, reeducation.

Detailing White Ignorance and a Need for Reeducation

White Americans experience life with minimal considerations of race because the system was created for White people, and societal learning revolves around Whiteness, granting them the privilege or, rather, the exemption of learning about other racial groups (Bell et al., 2016). According to antiracist essayist Tim Wise, African Americans "have to know White knowledge, White wisdom, and what their experience is, but White people don't have to know the experiences of [Black people]" (Siek, 2011, para. 11). When it comes to race, White people are nescient, meaning they lack what is to others common knowledge, as their existence never necessitates a need for that knowledge. Nothing about the average White existence compels or even encourages an exploration into anything other than accepted White culture.

This matter of White ignorance was made personally poignant and clear to me when I was asked to sit on an expert panel to discuss "Race Based Trauma & Mental Health: A Conversation of Understanding" during the "Racial Awakening" of 2020. This panel was hosted by a predominantly White university in rural Illinois as a part of an institutional effort to foster racial understanding. The initial prompt was for each of the Black panelists to tell the audience about a single incident of race-based trauma. My answer seemed to stun the White panelists. I responded accordingly.

> Black people don't have incidents of racial trauma; we exist in racial trauma. We experience racism and the subsequent trauma as early as we can walk and talk. Then, we are placed in educational systems that think that the contributions of Black people are limited to Dr. Martin Luther King, Rosa Parks, and Harriet Tubman, all while glorifying the savagery of Christopher Columbus. That same system would place us in handcuffs at age eight but assigns a White youth an individualized education program or (IEP). And, so we are fighting this system [of racism] internalizing our own trauma to achieve some semblance of success. And, after 11 years of post-secondary education, four degrees, and 30+ certifications, all at a price tag of a quarter of a million dollars, we are sat aside from a [White] colleague who tells us the only reason we are employed by the University is because we are Black … We lay our heads down at night, hoping that as our heavy heads hit a cold pillow that physical relief will translate into relief from this trauma. And, we pray to

> our Creator for providence and protection, not protection from the vagabond, gangster, thug, or criminal; but protection from a racist policing system that will shoot us eight times in our sleep … I guess I respond to your question with a question: how does one, whose very existence evokes racism, only identify one incident of racial trauma? (SIU System, 2020, 23:24–26:07).

It was the White panelists' response to this opening oration that clearly demonstrated that White people rarely, if ever, consider the lived experiences of Black people, admitting that they lost count of the differing types of racial trauma explained in an oration that was not even three minutes long, even though the experiences are not uncommon to most Black people. One White panelist thanked the Black panelists for their willingness to "teach us," acknowledging that privilege creates a life for White Americans where they never have to consider race. In a moment of unexpected candor, this White panelist admitted that White people know little outside of Whiteness.

However, the central theme of White ignorance regarding the experiences of Black people that this book attempts to use as a conversation primer is not a new observance but one that racial activists have been championing for decades. More than fifty years ago, Dr. Martin Luther King, Jr. eloquently said: "It must be frankly said [White people] are not putting in a similar effort to reeducate themselves out of their racial ignorance. It is an aspect of their sense of superiority that the White people of America believe they have so little to learn" (King, 1967). Dr. King not only confirms the racial ignorance at the center of faulty defenses like, "I have Black friends," but he also presents an additional probable cause — a racist sense of inherent preeminence. Dr. King's assertion is not to be confused with disadvantageous laziness, which may characterize why some Whites are comfortably accepting of the poverty of other White persons. They accept what they believe to be the undeniable truth that some inequity will exist, and they are indolent in their actions. However, the ignorance Dr. King spoke of refers to the unwillingness to support, learn of, or even acknowledge anything not centering on White Eurocentric culture based on empty notions of racial supremacy — a cognition that can be adopted by poor White people as well.

Scholars after Dr. King affirmed similar notions. Twenty years after Dr. King articulated this, Cardell Jacobson (1985) called it "new racism," or a racial thought process rooted in White self-interest. Jacobson's peer-reviewed study demonstrated that White interest prevented the learning and support of policies and political positions as they culturally did not want to engage in any practice that did not center on Whiteness. Jacobson's study further invalidates the White claim for racial exoneration by having Black friends, as the White person likely has little to no knowledge of what it means to be Black beyond seeing dark skin, because such knowledge would not promote White-group interests.

Therefore, when White people defend their accusations of racism with Black proximity, the defense's illegitimacy is evident as they have little, and often inaccurate, knowledge of what it means to be Black in America. White racial privilege, rooted in a false sense of superiority, allows them to "move through the world with an expectation that their needs be readily met," with no consideration that others' needs go unmet (Collins, 2018, 3). The America of White privilege makes Black experiences irrelevant, and the defense of having Black friends or family is only relevant as a defense of self-declared White morality!

Additionally, when I reference privilege, I am not inferring an exemption from hardship but unearned advantages systemically granted (Collin, 2018). Privilege is not the absolution from common life difficulties. It is, however, common and often unnoticed conveniences, benefits, and comforts that are exclusive to White people. For example, White people do not have to look for White hair-care aisles in stores because the client whom mainstream hair-care brands make their products for are not the customers with textured hair. White people never have to consider that their race alone may be the reason for harassment by law enforcement. They never have to remove family pictures from homes so that their property will be appraised appropriately, nor do they have to worry that their name sounds too *urban* when applying for a job. And this privilege allows White people to never consider their own racial advantages or the disadvantageous realities of racial minorities.

The racial detachment between White and Black Americans is proven by data — only 36 percent of White people, approximately one in every three, believe that racial discrimination prevents Black progress, according to a 2016 Pew Research Center Study on Race and Inequality. The ignorance and detachment are so severe that when the same study posed questions as to the cause of the persistent Black-White gap in household income, more than half of White Americans believed that this sixty-plus-year inequity was because of a lack of good role models available to Black people — an opinion affirmed while a Black family with Ivy League educations occupied the White House, the Obamas. Not only is there an ignorance substantiated by data, but the resistance to reeducation that Dr. King spoke of is also evinced by data, as the same Pew Research study found that 41 percent of White respondents felt "too much attention" was being paid to racial issues. Not during Reconstruction, nor the Civil Rights Era, but currently, contemporary public opinion is that almost half of White people feel there is nothing for them to learn regarding race.

Outline of the Book

This book serves as a primer or conversation starter in the reeducation of race by posing a different inquisition to the reader in each chapter about their understanding of race as it relates to Black Americans. Each question/chapter title is then answered in the chapter using a unique combination of information sources, including historiographies, public opinion data, and peer-reviewed literature. This question-and-answer format was chosen, as it makes the book more than a survey of the Black experience — it is an instruction starter on the inherently discriminatory system of race that (1) shows the readers their own ignorance, (2) provides an initial foundation of knowledge, and (3) places the responsibility for dismantling discriminatory systems on those most privileged by the system of race. This book's unique and primary data source is an exclusive set of interviews by transgenerational Black Americans who detail unfiltered lifelong narratives of the Black experiences collected under Institutional Review Board (IRB) Protocol #1757. These transgenerational Black Americans have experienced the hierarchy of race across multiple generations and in multiple legal racialized systems — having clear cognitive memories before the legalization of racial integration — making them the ideal instructors in this reeducation.

Chapter 2, "Do You Know What Makes Us Black?" continues one theme from this introductory chapter — affirming that any notion of race solely based on skin tone and individual visible features is an incomplete understanding of race. The chapter discusses race as a social construct in which biological distinctions serve only as cues to who should receive certain sociopolitical rights. The chapter begins with the truthful historiography of Sarah Rector, a Black teen who, though biologically Black, was legally deemed White because a unique set of circumstances placed her beyond the disadvantageous tier shared by Black Americans of the time. Using the historical account of Sarah Rector, the chapter reveals there are factors beyond skin color key in race's construction, yet there are systemic motives that attempt to sustain a narrative rooted in biological differences that do not match the experiential narrative of being racialized as Black.

Building from this case, this chapter provides a three-part definition of "Black" that draws in part from Lori Gallegos de Castillo's (2018) discussion of unconscious racial prejudice. This definition decenters biological similarities and recenters Black as an "identity rooted in discrimination and disadvantage based on false narratives" — false narratives because of a privileged refusal to learn past skin and, in turn, invent the character of Black people, drawing implication from the peer-reviewed research of Lewis and Nelson (2021). The chapter then validates this experience-based definition by showing that it accurately characterizes the Black existence across the five major racial labels of Black people — "African slave," "Colored," "Negro," "Black," and "African American." This chapter establishes that being racialized as Black has less to do with considerations than skin color and more to do with systemic shortcomings of a society designed to sustain White privilege.

Building on the racial ignorance asserted in chapter 2, chapter 3, titled "Do You Know That's Not Anger, It's Trauma?" addresses a common stereotype perpetuated about Black Americans — anger. This chapter begins by showing that ordinary actions of Black Americans are deemed hostile and angry because the stereotype benefits inaction on the part of White systems. Also the stereotype delegitimizes any claim of racial prejudice experienced by Black people. In an additional effort to correct misunderstandings of Blackness, the chapter affords the central premise that the observed emotional frustration White people witness is, in actuality, racial trauma. The chapter uses Eve Carlson's discussion of trauma to develop a framework to assess whether Black people are violently angry and hostile or if they have legitimate emotional responses to racism as a traumatic experience.

This chapter introduces the racialized narratives of transgenerational African Americans. Using the information from the selected interviews alongside the framework developed in the chapter presents strong evidence that the discriminatory experiences that shape Blackness are a shared trauma. By default, this chapter disproves the common stereotype that Blacks are angry, as in hostile or violent, as being Black means a continued existence of racial trauma with little, if any, relief.

Chapter 4, "Do You Know that the Institutions that Serve You Destroy Us?" continues the reeducation of the book by informing on how institutions are culpable in the disadvantageous outcomes of a racialized system. The chapter accepts the premise of James Baldwin (1967) that interpersonal race relations cannot improve without an improvement in institutional racial equity, as institutions are a reflection of interpersonal racial realities. After providing evidence that institutional distrust is thematic to those racialized as Black, this chapter does a comprehensive case study of policing as an institution to demonstrate that American institutions were designed, sustained, and cultivated to respond differently to Black citizens. This chapter then uses an appropriate narrative from the collection of transgenerational interviews to show how institutional mistreatment can exist despite legal reforms. In sum, this chapter demonstrates that the disadvantageous nature of race cannot solely be remedied by individual actions, as institutional restructuring will also be a necessary component.

Chapter 5, "Do You Know Black Youth Are Robbed of Healthy Childhoods?" continues to chronicle an experiential discussion of race by showing that the inherent disadvantages of a racialized system impose mistreatment on Black youth even before Black youth are conscious of such disadvantage. The chapter reproves the pervasive nature of racism referenced in earlier chapters and demonstrates how racism robs Black children of a childhood comparable to their White counterparts. This chapter begins by revealing the more commonly known narrative that overt racism robs Black youth of life, particularly Black males from George Stinney to Emmett Till to Trayvon Martin to Tamir Rice, drawing heavily on the exposition of Quaylan Allen and Henry Metcalf (2019) that situates the intersection of racism and hypermasculinity imposed on Black male youth. However, this chapter goes beyond evincing that the inescapable nature of racism robs Black youth of life. It addresses how racism robs meaningful childhood experiences from Black youth whose lives are not ended by overt racism.

Chapter 5 also shows that the racial experiences common to Black people handicap Black parenting by placing parents in a perpetual loop of stress-induced survivalism — a narrative articulated by James Baldwin (1964). This chapter introduces another interview from the collection of transgenerational Black citizens to show how the stories of past racism are shared within the

Black family as a form of protectionism to equip Black youth for current inevitable encounters of racism. However, this introduction of Black trauma focused on ensuring survival restricts the curious exploration of childhood needed for healthy emotional and intellectual maturation.

Chapter 6, "Do You Know that Black 'Hard Work' Is Not the Answer?" preemptively addresses a likely counterpoint to be asserted by non-Black readers, if they have not already disengaged from the material — the counternarrative of hard work. In a racial context, many default to a narrative that the depressed conditions that the average Black person experiences can be overcome if Black people simply work harder. This narrative has been consistently demonstrated by a particular question of racial resentment asked in the American National Election Study questionnaire for decades. To no surprise, a plurality of White people believe the disadvantageous reality Black people face can be overcome if Black people simply work harder. Not only does this position evince another stereotype imposed on Black people (that is, laziness), but, more importantly, it is a false presupposition. In a racialized system, one cannot work themselves out of oppression — a notion discussed by Darrick Hamilton et al. (2015).

This chapter draws a clear distinction between individual attainment and the inherent systemic discrimination experienced by Black Americans. It shows that even as some Black people attain measures of success, those accomplishments do not mitigate racial oppression. They were achieved in spite of racial oppression and are not the common life experience for Black Americans. This chapter pulls from the life narratives of another interviewee whose life clearly shows that hard work may lead to some individual conveniences but does not negate the prejudicial treatment assigned in a racial hierarchy.

Finally, I pose the question of responsibility to the reader in light of the indisputable evidence that race is more than biological differences, as, by design, it assigns privilege to one group and oppression to others. The final chapter, "Do You Know It's Not Black People's Responsibility to Fix This?" follows the tradition of contemporary race scholarship by ending with remedial actions White individuals and White-constructed systems can take to achieve racial equity, similar to Claudine Turner and Liz Grauerholz's (2017) study of racism faced by Black men in higher education. This chapter begins by reminding the readers of the disadvantages and experiences common to Black people and informs them that there is little responsibility toward Black people, as they did not create the present systems of race and racism, and it should not be the responsibility of Black people to dismantle such systems. However, the tradition of Black remedial articulation of racism is as old as the problem of racism in the United States, going back to the abolition days of Frederick Douglass. Therefore, this chapter challenges the White reader to act in "allyship" to dismantle racism, as outlined by Helena Liu (2020). The framework for racial allyship suggested in this chapter was developed by this author in conjunction with sociologist Elizabeth Stygar — a multidisciplinary approach to changing systems through a process of reeducation. It challenges White people, as the racial group with the most racial privilege, to dismantle the systems of inequity or stop using the defense of "Black friends." Though the defense is not legitimate, how can a person affirm a friendship that is rooted in mistreatment?

An Initial Consideration in Priming a White Reeducation

Even though White claims of Black friends and family are without merit as a defense to accusations of racism, there is a heaviness in the phrase, "I have Black friends," of which the White speaker is also ignorant. When a White person desperately pronounces the phrase, what are they considering in the assertion of "Black?" If the US government's definition of Black, pulled from the US Census Bureau, is an indicator of how White people see race, which it likely is since White people composed the definition, then we get a glimpse into what White people mean by Black friends.

The US Census (2022) simply defines a Black person as "a person having origins in any of the Black racial groups of Africa." First, this catchall definition is insulting to the cultural and ethnic diversity of the African continent. Africa is the second-largest continent, with fifty-four countries, hundreds of tribal cleavages, and nearly 2,000 linguistic differences. Yet, in a dismissive way, anyone originating from the continent of Africa is lumped together by the US government. The definition adds insult to injury because it aggregates the diversity of Africa around the commonality of hue — understood by the definition's phrase "Black racial groups." The US government deems anyone from this diverse place as Black simply because most of these persons exhibit tiny genetic differences surrounding the enzyme tyrosinase, which, for them, functions at full capacity, producing more melanin and resulting in darker skin (Wills, 1994). Lumping hundreds of millions of people from hundreds of ethnicities together because of biological similarities creates the problem in the phrase "I have Black friends," as it misinforms that race is only a difference in skin color. This definition, and the White sociopolitical structure that accepts it, doesn't take race into consideration beyond visible biological distinctions.

However, one does not need to traverse decades in history to understand that while race includes biological references, it rests on sociopolitical and legal advantages/disadvantages, experiences, and realities created by a White power structure. A recent example was revealed by Freddie Mac — a congressionally charted home loan mortgage corporation. In 2021, Freddie Mac found that homes owned by Black people were appraised at significantly lower values than similar homes in White tracts or geographic locales. The rigor of the Freddie Mac study is that it debunks the "few bad apples" claim, as Section 3 of the study provides statistical evidence that most of the appraisers who performed appraisals in Black and White tracks produced "Black versus White gaps." In other words, the disadvantageous outcomes experienced by Black homeowners were not a result of individual actors but a system that conferred different experiences based on visible differences of the homeowner. The Freddie Mac study is a recent and clear example that most White people only consider skin color when thinking about race because the institutions of society only consider this. However, a skin-color-only understanding of race is an incomplete understanding!

The White defendant, who claims Black friends, is only concerned with defending their own perceived innocence. In their privilege, it is expectantly deemed reasonable that they are trustworthy and morally good, and accusations of being racist are an infringement on that moral self-view. In their hasty and empty defense, they have not considered that their declaration of proximity to Blackness is only a declaration of proximity to melanin. They've had to learn nothing about their "Black friend" except that their skin tones are different!

Being Black is not simply dark rich skin, an enlarged and round nasal cavity, and a distinctive eye orbit, but being Black is to live under societal and cultural paradigms that support notions of supposed inferiority. As a matter of fact, that was the entire point of the creation of racial categories in the United States. The US created race as a way to categorize people and specifically "justify the socio-economic arrangement that benefit[ed] the White racial group" (Bell et al., 2016, 133). Put another way, race in the US was created with the intentional purpose of sustaining privilege for British colonists who, in words, wanted to escape a system of tyranny but only wished to create a society where they were the tyrants. It is what Isabel Wilkerson called the caste system in which Black people, then enslaved Africans, were "firmly at the bottom" (2020, 45). And this caste system or hierarchy of benefits for the newly constructed racial category of White people ensured Black subjugation with a "labyrinth of laws" disproportionately written, disproportionately enforced, and disproportionately applied (Wilkerson, 2020, 48).

Today, the web of legal and sociopolitical structures that subjugate Black Americans has been retrofitted, but it is still characterized by discrimination leading to segregated and underfunded schools, a racialized school-to-prison pipeline, a presumption of criminality in shopping, aversive racism in hiring and promotion, and medical malpractice stemming from myths of eugenics. So, when one moves beyond biology when considering race, they can see that race is a social, political, and legal mechanism of societal placement with Black people reduced to the lowest possible designation of the citizenry, historically not being citizens or not even legally being human.

Chapter 2

"Do You Know What Makes Us Black?"

"With all the traits and characteristics of an Afro-American she has too much money and must be White." This was a line published in the newspaper article, "Brown Skinned Colored Girl Made White," in the November 15, 1913 printing of *The Chicago Defender*. The "Afro-American" referenced in this quote was Sarah Rector, a Black girl born in the Creek Indian Territory of Oklahoma, likely because her grandparents were Creek Freedmen — meaning they were slaves owned by the Creek Nation who were not freed under the Thirteenth Amendment but were granted emancipation under Article 2 of the 1866 US Treaty with the Creek Nation. Sarah was classified as a Creek Freedman, and under Article 3 of the Treaty, she and her Black siblings were granted land in the former West half of the Creek Nation territory.

However, because of the discriminatory nature of race discussed in the previous chapter, Sarah was given land of no agricultural value to which the local government could still make money because of exorbitant property taxes. The Rector family, a Black family still hobbled by the residual effects of slavery, could not afford the property taxes, which is why Sarah's father sought to sell the land. However, there was a unique network of laws that were discriminatory. The seemingly reparative effort was discriminatory in that: (1) it only gave land allotments to Black and Indigenous persons that seemingly had no value; and (2) once under the ownership of Black and Indigenous people, there was a time restraint to prevent reselling the land to prevent any monetary acquisitions and compel the collection of high property taxes. This meant that Sarah Rector was the legal owner of land she had likely never seen. It was land she could not cultivate, develop, or sell, yet the land made money for the White local government in Oklahoma through property taxes.

According to the *Oklahoma Star* (as cited by Diggs [1976]), the land allocated to Black youth by the Treaty was placed under White guardianship "appointed by the county courts of Oklahoma." White guardians automatically received 10 percent of profits from their work as guardians. But Sarah's land was initially seen as a throwaway. However, the inequitable allocation of land to Sarah, intended to be discriminatory, would benefit her, as oil was discovered on her land. T. J. Porter, Sarah's assigned White guardian, leased the oil-rich lands to B. B. Jones, as the law meant to be discriminatory to landowners forbade him from selling the land. Sarah's 90 percent share was to be held in trust, which would prove to make the youth extremely rich, as by the end of 1913, the profits were estimated at just under $15,000 a month (Diggs, 1976).

Figure 2.1. Sarah Rector. *Source*: Public domain.

But how could a Black person, particularly a Black preteen, have this type of money? The oil on Sarah's land made her, a Black girl, wealthier than any White girl in the Midwest. And the question before a racist White state was: How could a Black girl only a few decades from slavery be richer than arguably all the White people in Oklahoma? Such a reality could not exist in a racial system built on White advantage. The answer was to re-racialize Sarah Rector. Even with dark skin and the physical features common among Black people, within the limits of Oklahoma, Sarah was no longer considered Black. She was legally declared White and given the privileges of White people, such as riding in the front train car. *The Chicago Defender* wrote and articulated the White mindset concerning Sarah Rector's situation in a most unapologetic way.

> The White people have become so alarmed at the enormous wealth of the young girl that they do not like such wealth belonging to a girl of Afro-American blood.... But the politicians are becoming so stirred up that they [seek to make] her White by passing a law to that effect.... It's the same old idea of the White man that whenever a Negro achieves any distinction, either in scientific or literary world, some White men want to declare them White. (*The Chicago Defender*, November 15, 1913)

The exposition written about the mindset of White Americans at that time demonstrates one thing clearly — there are nonbiological components to race. If Sarah Rector's racial classification was changed because she no longer occupied the oppressed state society had placed on Black people, then Dr. Bell's and Dr. Middleton's characterization of race as a social construct, mentioned in the previous chapter, is correct. Race is about placement in a society where biological similarities are only cues of such placement, especially if the biological similarities shared by White people keep them in the most advantageous placement. However, the quote from *The Chicago Defender* is even more telling in that it reveals that the primary nonbiological component of race for those who are classified as Black is to be in a state of disadvantage and deprivation. It informs that if Black achievement persists, even if by simple good fortune in the face of the discriminatory system of race (as was the case of Sarah Rector), the individual cannot carry the racial designation of Black because, in a racialized system, the expectation is for Black to be synonymous to inferiority.

By 1914, Sarah's money led her to no longer be racialized as Black, at least in Oklahoma, and the rules preventing people with dark skin, kinky hair, and rounded nasal cavities from riding in the first-class train car no longer applied to Sarah. She was biologically Black, but socially and legally, she was White. Sarah Rector's story is a classic example that clearly elucidates that it is more than one's dark skin that makes one Black. The question becomes: What are those other things?

What Makes Us Black?

We learn from the actions of the Oklahoma legislature regarding Sarah Rector that being racialized is a passive act and has less to do with rigid categories based solely on visible differences in skin color. The categories of race rely heavily on baseless assumptions of worthlessness and false narratives of inferiority. The commonality of skin color that Sarah shared with other Black freedmen was only relevant as it was supposed to signal her inferiority. Sarah Rector, because of her dark skin, was expected to be poor, uneducated, and disenfranchised, and she was expected to remain there. Even when granted land, she was given land that White society saw as having no value except to benefit a White system through the enforcement of property taxes. Yet, when Sarah, by good fortune, found herself beyond the status of poverty in which she was supposed to remain, she was re-racialized and her biological commonalities with other Black free persons became irrelevant in Oklahoma.

The case study of Sarah Rector reveals the unspoken verity of racialized societies — skin color is only relevant to the power group because it communicates where individuals should be in terms of societal placement, and by default, it makes any investigation into learning about the humanity of those persons unnecessary. In simpler words, a focus on skin color or any external characteristic allows the controlling group the unfair privilege to prematurely determine the level of disadvantage others should experience and remain ignorant of any real experiences. They do not have to learn, yet they can make determinations in that ignorance. Additionally, if the racial society limits information to visible distinctions, it allows the members of society to fill in all other information with assumptions and stereotypes and even use the falsified information to sustain oppression while simultaneously sustaining their own racial advantage. In the American racialized system, biotics are the designated information of importance because they allow White people to make assumptions about income, residency, occupation, educational attainment, guilt versus innocence, and even speech articulation of those with non-White biotics.

This is often played out when historically minoritized people obtain high-level reputable occupations (CEOs, university presidents, etcetera). When they obtain these positions, White people often assume they were unqualified and only attained the position through some social justice version of affirmative action; this happens because the non-White person's skin color, hair texture, and other visible characteristics allow White people to assume their credentials, no matter the depth of their qualifications (Pitman, 2012). In addition to allowing ignorant presumptions, a focus on skin color allows White people to fill in missing information with myths, distortions, and lies that justify racial discrimination and mistreatment of Black people. In the United States, if the only information White people have to know is color, then they believe themselves justified in determining the rest. If White society determines the rest as unimportant, they are justified in their dismissive dehumanization; if they determine the rest as incapable, they are justified in their denial of resources; and if they determine the rest as dangerous, they are justified in their violence.

Understanding this paradigm, a more accurate definition of Black, one that is more comprehensive than the definition offered by the US Census Bureau, is a person in the global group whose visual distinctions are most opposite to those of European origin, for whom White active ignorance determines a sociopolitical identity rooted in discrimination and disadvantage based on false narratives. This definition has three components. The first is visual distinctions most opposite European origin. Europeans tend to have a melanin deficiency, resulting in pale skin, "long narrow noses and visible cheekbones," among other shared physical features (University of Pittsburgh, 2024). It should be made clear that the visual distinctions here are not a reference to phrenology. Phrenology is the notion that observed biological differences are an indication of ability, and this definition does not even infer natural ability based on these biological differences (Obasogie, 2017).

In addition, promulgations and even inferences that there are genomic differences between races only legitimize the unfounded core principles of eugenics. Therefore, when one conceptualizes Black, it is only about the perceptible, or seen, differences—upon observation, those racialized as Black have visible features most differing from those designated as White. These visible features of skin color and hair texture should be perceived as "nothing more than a neutral variation in human appearance" (Wilkerson, 2020, 42). However, these differences inform a White power structure of who merits an inquisition of additional information on their part. It justifies a centering of themselves to the degree that they can remain resistantly ignorant about others. Thus, it is not ignorance because of a lack of access to information but an ignorance of avoiding information (de Castillo, 2018). This is called active ignorance.

This active ignorance is the second component. When visible distinctions align with the features most opposite those of European origin, it serves as a signal that there is no need to learn anything about the real existence of those persons. It is a conscious choice not to learn if we recall Dr. King's words from the previous chapter. However, it is common knowledge, or assumed to be common knowledge, that humans fill in the missing information. For example, our brains perform phonemic restoration when audible parts of a speech are missing and can even fill in optics when we blink. This cognitive ability functions similarly when "active ignorance" is engaged or when persons refuse to learn about the differences of others — the mind fills that incomplete information in.

By now, you, the reader, have reasoned that the problem with filling in information from active ignorance is that the information is more likely than not incomplete, inaccurate, or completely false. Black people are the recipients of the false or baseless narratives that White people impose on them. This false information, because of resistance to go beyond skin color, manifests itself through institutions and individuals. Lori Gallegos de Castillo (2018) informs us that one false narrative may be that Black people are untrustworthy, and this is why police investigators may doubt the eyewitness testimonies of Black witnesses. This falsehood goes back to Reconstruction, where in some states, such as Kentucky, Black witnesses could only testify if no White witnesses were available, as it is presumed that their testimony was more trustworthy (Kaczorowski, 1987).

Beyond de Castillo's example, other common false narratives are that Black persons are inherently unintellectual, which is why Black graduate students, even professors, often have their intellect questioned or their employment reduced to some affirmative action initiative. Several examples are detailed in Dr. Shardé Davis's book, *Being Black in the Ivory: Truth-Telling About Racism in Higher Education*. And, even Black business professionals are automatically suspected of illegal activity because of the false narrative that assumes all Black people are poor and live in ghettos. These false narratives may even question Black morals although Black Americans exhibit higher levels of religiosity and ethical salience than White people. In essence, an entire false framework of information is assigned to the entire group of people with shared visible distinctions because there is no willingness to learn facts beyond the visible skin color.

The White skeptic is likely ready to refute the definition's third component — a discriminatory existence. First, White skeptics must relinquish the delusion that racism, like an ominous odor, dissipates over time, and because there has been some racial progress, racial discrimination is not systemic. The manifestations or outcomes of racism reveal that racism is systemic, and Black Americans are currently dealing with some of the same issues that have been pervasive for centuries. In 1787, the original US Constitution dehumanized Black people as only three-fifths of a person, and that dehumanization persists, because a Black person with a gun is a thug and a threat, but a White person with a gun is enjoying constitutional liberty granted by the Second Amendment. In 1852, Black people were more likely to get the death penalty than White people, and current estimates are that 55 percent of those currently on death row are Black or Brown, according to the American Civil Liberties Union (2003). Up until Reconstruction, the slave patrol was the leading cause of death for Black people, and the police (discussed in chapter 4) is birthed from the slave patrol and is still a leading cause of death for Black men (Edwards et al., 2019). The discriminatory existence in which Black people have existed still largely characterizes what it means to be Black. This was at the core of sociopolitical research conducted by myself and political scientist Dr. Sherice J. Nelson.

Dr. Nelson and I understood the active ignorance that saturated society, which became inconspicuous following 2020, as many White conservatives voiced false narratives about the global protests following the deaths of Ahmaud Arbery, Breanna Taylor, and George Floyd. These false narratives were repeated by a small minority of controversial Black conservatives, like commentator Candace Owens, who voiced that protestors were immorally disrupting and inconveniencing orderly life. This mostly White group filled in the missing information with falsehoods, even calling the protestors "chimpanzees." However, this active ignorance has existed for decades, if not centuries, before that racial awakening of 2020. Still, it was the 2019 tweet by African American actor Isaiah Washington, likely most famous for his role as Dr. Preston Burke on *Grey's Anatomy*, that served as a spark for our research.

Washington tweeted that he believed that "President Trump had done more for Black people than Obama" — a statement that was inconsistent with the majority of Black Americans opinions of the two presidents. The opinion of Washington prompted Nelson and me to question: How can a person who identifies as African American, sharing undeniable biological similarities, find themself so ideologically opposed to the Black collective?

Dr. Nelson's initial response to Washington became the basis for our study. She stated, "Those of us insulated enough from the system speaking … personal truths that in no way reflect the experiences of our people as a whole." Nelson's response centered on the experiential component of race. She speculated that Washington's opinion was rooted in the perception, true or not, that his infamy insulated him from the racist experiences common to Black people. To investigate this plausible experiential component, we used respondent data from the 2016 American National Election Study (ANES), assessing the responses of more than 2,400 Black citizens. We immediately find that of the experiences frequently investigated in studies of race, racial discrimination is the most frequent for Black Americans. Approximately 73 percent of Black Americans did not possess a bachelor's degree, and another 81 percent had an annual income of less than $75,000, with identical percentages noting religious importance. Yet 91 percent of Black citizens noted a personal experience of racial discrimination. There was no experience documented more frequently for Black Americans than racism. However, the study goes beyond reporting percentages.

We use the response data to implement a regression analysis — a statistical technique that can help determine how much, or to what degree some phenomena change others. The regression output showed that experiences of racial discrimination shape the perspectives of those who identify as Black across a variety of sociopolitical issues, including affirmative action in education. To determine how impactful racism is, predicted probabilities were computed to understand how increases in racism shape the Black identity. It was found that racism not only occurs frequently but it is significantly impactful. For example, Black respondents who are neutral regarding affirmative action, neither supporting nor opposing, are 15 percent more likely to show some support when they have a moderate number of racist experiences. In short, Dr. Nelson and I empirically show that discrimination plays a greater significance in being racialized as Black than shared visible cues, because there is no experience more common and arguably more impactful than racism.

Again, anticipating rebuttals from skeptics of this redefining of the Black racial group, I know the counterargument that using my own research is an ideal example of author bias. I direct the skeptic to the work of Dr. Sharon Wright Austin. Dr. Austin surveyed 2,359 Black Americans from different ethnic or cultural origins, including African Americans, and Black ethnic citizens from Cape Verde, Haiti, and the West Indian Islands. Her research found that all Black people, whether African American or ethnically Black, shared a racial group consciousness resulting from "their common experiences with racial discrimination" (Austin, 2018, 8–9). To the disputer of this definition and my efforts to support it with my own published research, how would you argue against the rigorous research of Dr. Austin, whose findings provide stronger evidence as she studies a larger and more ethnically diverse group of non-White persons? Yet she still discovered that "most African Americans and first- and second-generation Black ethnics identify as Black," because "their position is disadvantaged by American racism" (Austin, 2018, 158).

Being Black, according to the exegesis of historical events, like the case of Sarah Rector, and social science research, like that of Dr. Sharon Austin, describes the group possessing visual distinctions most opposite to those of European origin, for whom White ignorance permits false narratives or incomplete information to situate this group in a system of discrimination and disadvantage. But are these cherry-picked points selected for the creation of the author's desired narrative? Is the author picking evidence to support his constructed definition, including his own peer-reviewed research? To further substantiate the legitimacy of this definition, one only needs to determine if the definition is applicable to Black people across the different racial labels historically. Black Americans have gone through a variety of racial labels, and perhaps this definition would be acceptable to the contrarian if it holds up at every point in the Black existence in America across these labels.

Label Be Damned

Black Americans have not always been identified by the racial label of "Black." The racial label, or the social and political descriptor assigned to the group, has been fluid even though the changing label references the same racial group — the group in America with visible physical features most opposite Europeans in this country. However, the definition of Black people offered in this chapter accurately explains the sociopolitical reality of the Black experience despite the racial labels used to describe the group, as the change in label was often more symbolic, rarely representing a lessening of discrimination or oppression. A historical examination of the labels assigned to and accepted by Black Americans shows that there are five prominent racial labels: "African Slave," "Colored," "Negro," "Black," and "African American."

African Slave

Before growing talks of emancipation began to swell in the mid-1800s, African slaves were clearly characterized as a group distinctively opposite White people upon simple observation. The clearest distinction is what Isabel Wilkerson (2020) calls a melanated "birthmark over [the] entire body." Many White slavers, politicians, and scientists saw this as an opportunity to animalize African slaves — a baseless defense to justify their dehumanization of sentencing this group to perpetual enslavement. And as the definition of Black offered here informs, the differences in appearance allowed active ignorance of the White people. Whites "absorbed, digested and regurgitated" baseless claims of natural inferiority (Quallen, 2016, 50). This resistant ignorance led to false narratives, primarily narratives that the African slave was immoral and needed social and legal control.

This false narrative was exposed in the courageous oration of Fredrick Douglass, "What to the Slave Is the Fourth of July?" Douglass explained that the law sought to regulate the African slave while giving little to no regulation to White people, as White people had used the law to declare themselves morally good under the presumption that the African slave possessed no moral compass. Douglass evinces this by pointing out that in 1852, the State of Virginia had seventy-two capital offenses that governed African slaves and only two for White people. This racial-legal imbalance showed the untruthfulness that had been imposed on the slave, because if slaves could comply with seventy-two capital offenses in a dehumanizing legal structure, while White persons only needed to comply with two, would that not make the slaves more moral than White persons? This false narrative expresses that African slaves were insolent and insubordinate and only forceful dehumanizing treatment and the hard handof the law could quell such immorality, according to Guy B. Johnson (1939). Additionally, it shows how race is a discriminatory social construct, as the law itself assigned differing treatment.

Figure 2.2. Prominent Racial Labels for Black Americans, 1800–2023. *Note*: Other racial labels, such as "Afro-American," were used historically. However, these labels represent the most commonly used ones, and the time placement represents the most confident overlap of use by a majority of Black persons (Smith, 1992), with the exception of "African Slave" and official use as a label by the US Census Bureau at some point (US Office of Management and Budget, 2010). *Source*: Created by the author.

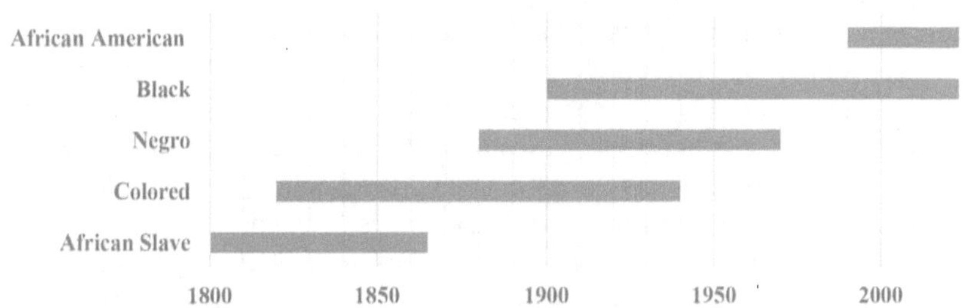

Colored

Even before the abolition of slavery, free Black persons were identified under the racial label of "Colored." According to Smith (1994), the racial label "Colored" covered "mulattoes and others of mixed racial ancestry as well as those with complete Black ancestry" (497). This is likely because when Congress passed the 1808 "Act Prohibiting the Importation of Slaves" (signed in 1807) — a compromise of the Constitutional Convention in 1787 (Article 1, Section 9) — the language of the law stated: "any negro, mulatto, or person of color" (Malesky, 2014). Thus, persons now labeled as Black affirmed the label of "Colored" as it was the most acceptable term for White people. Reminding us that the affirmations of Dr. Richard Middleton (2008) were true, as the nuisance of mixed-race people was irrelevant because their visible features did not reflect European origin.

However, discussing that this is the group most visually distinct from White persons is of little impact, as slavery is still a prevalent practice and growing, and even free "Colored" persons had to show papers to prove they were not fugitive slaves. And, in this dynamic is the active ignorance proven, as it created false narratives leading to a discriminatory existence. The slave patrol often dismissed the need to properly investigate the validity of freed claims made by "Colored" people at the time. Therefore, a free "Colored" person who had never been a slave could be enslaved through the unjust practices of capture by the slave patrol. All the White-run slave patrol needed to do was assert that based on similar looks, a free person was indeed an escaped slave. They had no need to make further inquiries to create the untruthful narrative that the free "Colored" person in question was the suspected escaped slave, and they could force slavery on someone who, by law, should have never endured the dehumanizing reality.

Negro

The active ignorance that White people used to create falsehoods leading to legal and social discrimination against the former slaves and free "Colored" men did not stop with the end of the Civil War, nor the passage of the Thirteenth, Fourteenth, and Fifteenth Amendments, even though the label of "Negro" was growing in popularity and outpacing the acceptability of "Colored." Black leaders emerging out of Reconstruction (1880s), such as Booker T. Washington and W. E. B. Du Bois, favored "Negro" as opposed to "Colored," even though some organizations still held on to the pre–Civil War label, such as the National Association for the Advancement of Colored People (NAACP) (Smith, 1994). However, even while Union soldiers occupied the South, we saw an increase in what would become known as the Black Codes (Toland, 2006). The Black Codes were legal and extralegal measures to ensure that Black people would never achieve equality or equity. The laws and norms sought to prevent Black people, then often referenced as "Negro," from receiving mortgages, loans, and voting, and sought to humiliate Black people in everyday life with statutes such as "sidewalk laws" — Black people had to give the right-of-way to White people on the sidewalk and do so in a way that pleased White people.

To understand the active ignorance and discrimination that Black people faced when referred to as "Negro," one only had to read the then-popular essay "Race Orthodoxy in the South" by Thomas Pearce Bailey. Bailey's essay set the "racial creed of Southern people," in which he noted that the "White race must dominate." And to achieve racial subordination, there could be "no social equality" and "no political equality" for Negroes. This racial reality fostered the resistant ignorance of many Whites, even Northern Whites, and prevented them from learning about the "Negro," beyond limited engagement in the cheating system of sharecropping. Because White people were actively ignorant of "Negros" and the inequitable system of the Black Codes, they created false narratives of Black persons (then "Negroes") as "inferior" (Wilkins et al., 2012, 17). This narrative led to the discriminatory use of the Black Codes along with the exception clause of the Thirteenth Amendment to, in essence, reenslave Black people. W. E. B. Du Bois writes of this: "[The country] was convinced of the impossibility of free Negro labor, the first and almost universal device was to use the courts as a means of reenslaving the Blacks. It was not a question of crime, but rather one of color, that settled a man's conviction on almost any charge" (Du Bois, 1903, 84). Because the Thirteenth Amendment allowed slavery as punishment for a crime and there was still a need for a workforce, White prejudice wrapped in the untruthful narratives of Negro inferiority placed Blacks back in a system of perpetual servitude.

Black

The label "Black" was used as early as 1900, most notably in the title of Du Bois's book, *The Souls of Black Folk*. However, it wasn't until the 1950s and 1960s that "Black" began to gain momentum as a racial label affirmed by both Black and White people. "Linguistically it was the best parallel to or match for 'White.' If 'White' was the proper racial label for that race, then it was argued that 'Black' was the proper term for the opposite race" (Smith, 1994, 501). Additionally, "Black" as a racial label began to evoke pride, power, and a rejection of the racist status quo; it was a detachment from the subservient implications of "Negro." As Black Americans embraced the racial label of "Black" and the spirit of resistance to racial oppression that it seemed to inspire, again because of a refusal of White people to learn about Black people or about the system Black people existed in, they created the false narrative that "Blacks" were evil, disruptive of order, destructive, and even hypocritical. The most famous example is the incarceration of Dr. Martin Luther King Jr. in 1963 in Birmingham, Alabama, from which he wrote the infamous *Letter from the Birmingham Jail*.

Dr. King went to Birmingham, Alabama from Atlanta, Georgia, hoping to pressure the city to integrate its restaurants and dining facilities through nonviolent protests, using the media to broadcast the entrenched segregation that existed in Alabama. Dr. King applied for a permit to protest, as was the law, but on April 10th, the city government obtained a state circuit court injunction against all protests. Two days later, on April 12th, Dr. King protested anyway, despite not having a permit, and he was incarcerated. Eight White evangelical ministers released a public statement condemning Dr. King and created a false narrative about his actions and the actions of activists nationwide: "We are convinced that these demonstrations are unwise and untimely ... such actions as incite to hatred and violence, however technically peaceful those actions may be" (*Statement by Alabama Clergymen, April 12, 1963*). The false narrative was that the Black efforts for equality and justice were not truthfully peaceful and only exacerbated racial hatred. This narrative was used to stall integration for as long as possible in several municipalities throughout the US, sustaining the discriminatory experiences of Black people.

African American

In the 1980s, there was a proposition that began in the Black urban centers to adopt "African American" as the racial label, even though by this time, both Black and White citizens, institutions, and even the government had affirmed the use of "Black." However, some Black leaders, like Jessie Jackson, wanted "to give Blacks a cultural identification with their heritage and ancestral homeland" (Smith, 1994, 507). However, this change in label did not necessarily produce a substantive shift in the treatment endured by Black Americans. During the 1980s, the narrative of conservative White citizens was that inner cities with a majority Black population were the eyesore of American life, and all such inner cities were filled with drugs and crime — a narrative from White people who never resided in the inner cities, such as former President Ronald Reagan.

However, dismissing that there were Black cities that thrived, like Atlanta, Georgia, Reagan championed the Anti-Drug Abuse Act of 1986 — a law designed to force the narrative of crime-ridden African American centers to be truthful through technical language that would lead to discriminatory incarceration rates. This law took into consideration the same drug, "crack," which was in both "African American" and White communities. Still, "crack cocaine" (mostly used in the Black community) was more criminal than "powder cocaine," which was used in the White communities. And according to studies from the University of Iowa, for every White person sentenced on a drug charge of powder cocaine, there were 100 Blacks sentenced for crack cocaine, even though it was the same drug. This extremely inequitable criminalization of "African Americans" led to reinforcing the false narrative that equated being Black with being a criminal.

Today, the racial labels "Black" and "African American" are often used interchangeably. But what is clear is that this group of citizens with visible features most opposite of those with Eurocentric features has a proven history of systemic discrimination based on false narratives, as White citizens have been actively ignorant to learn of them. During the label of "African slavery," the false narrative, among many, was that the African slave lacked any moral virtue, needing to be lorded over in a system of dehumanization. During the time when the label "Colored" was used, the false narrative was that "Colored" people were subhuman, meriting a return to slavery, and without control, this race of people would run amuck. When the label "Negro" was used, the false narrative was that Black people were inferior, despite prominent intellectuals such as Du Bois and Washington; thus, Negroes did not merit any place in society outside of servant or criminal. During the rise of the "Black" label, particularly its embrace by Black people during the Civil Rights era, the false narrative was that Black people were violent instigators with motives of hatred. And during the conservative reclamation of the 1980s, when the label of "African American" rose to notoriety, the narrative was, and arguably still is, that Black Americans were dangerous criminals — a return to a false narrative from 100 years ago.

Conclusion

The "Black friend" those accused of racism are so quick to claim to have, is not simply a friend with dark rich skin, an enlarged and round nasal cavity, and a distinctive eye orbit, but a friend whose legacy is survival, and sometimes unbelievable achievement, under societal, cultural, and legal paradigms that create a system of discrimination simply because White citizens, who are both the statistical and power majority, are resistantly ignorant and choose not to learn past skin color. And though the name/label of the racial group has changed, the history of discrimination, covert and overt, cannot be denied, even though it is often ignored.

I want to be clear that this chapter has gone to lengths not to define racism but to define race. This is important because many falsely conclude that race is a social construct that does not assign treatment and that it is racism or some manifestation of racial disdain that leads some to experience injustice and inequality. Throughout the history of the Black existence, their treatment was not solely determined by interpersonal racism but by their racialization, which designated that a certain treatment be imposed on them. Racism is the enforcement of race, as racism cannot exist without the hierarchy of race (Williams, 2023). It is those racial categories that assign experiential realities to groups, particularly with respect to the dominant group, which in the US is White people.

As we continue this reeducation about what it means to be racialized as Black, some will dismiss this chapter with the common stereotype of anger

— accusing my unapologetic articulation of Blackness as being angrily written, though it is not. In many discussions of race, there seems to be a propensity to dismiss truthful claims under the pretense that the Black orator is angry. The next chapter explores the dismissive stereotype of Black people as angry in this discussion of race. The chapter shows that the accusation of anger is a manifestation of White resistant ignorance. Anger would be justified; however, the chapter demonstrates that what is falsely labeled as anger is really the racial trauma carried from existing under the umbrella of race and the subsequent experiences of systemic racism. The upcoming chapter not only informs why the stereotype of Black anger was created and has been sustained, but it also reveals the lifetime trauma experienced by Black people while showing that claims of anger are without merit because most Black Americans hold no hostility toward White Americans. The next chapter poses the question: "Do you know that's not anger, it's trauma?"

Chapter 3

"Do You Know That's Not Anger, It's Trauma?"

> I remember my niece not long ago said, "You know, I'm being considered an angry Black woman pretty much at work because I don't go out and drink with my colleagues.... I don't drink, you know, and it makes me uncomfortable to be around people who drink.... I just want to be able to say, 'Hey, I'm not gonna go hang out with you guys. You all go ahead; I'll see you tomorrow at work,' without feeling like I'm judged or hearing later that I'm not a good, you know, team player."
>
> — Dr. Psyche Williams-Forson

The above quote was part of a larger online conversation between the hosts of *Gallup's Cultural Competence* podcast (Camille Loyd and Dr. Ella Washington) and Dr. Psyche Williams-Forson about food shame and the culture of food socializing in the workplace. Dr. Williams-Forson discusses how consuming food and social interactions around food consumption are cultural, meaning there are norms, beliefs, habits, and obviously cooking techniques associated with food, though some see it as a culturally absent social activity. During this conversation, Dr. Williams-Forsom recalls a conversation with her niece in which a simple decline to drink socially was, in this incident, justification for one of the most prominent stereotypes imposed on Black people — that we are angry. To bring consensus to the conversation, stereotypes are "overly generalized assumptions and beliefs about groups of people that are embedded in the dominant culture" (Adam and Zuniga, 2016, 99). Additionally, stereotypes are often reproduced and strengthened by individual attitudes and behaviors and are not easily changed in spite of factual evidence. One may say that stereotypes are enduring myths, which, because they are so salient, are accepted as true.

The Black "angry" stereotype, as with most beliefs about Black people, has roots in slavery, according to Rutgers University History Professor Dr. Deborah

Gray White (cited in the *Harvard Business Review* [2022]). Dr. White's assertion that the angry Black person stereotype was rooted in slavery was proven early in the century by Sterling Brown (1933). Brown was seeking to reveal what he called the "great injustice in American literature," which was the dismissive and unauthentic way Black people were stereotyped (180). Brown investigated literature as far back as 1832, and noted there were seven popular stereotypes placed on Black people: "the contented slave," "the wretched freeman," "the comic Negro," "the brute Negro," "the tragic mulatto," "the local-color Negro," and "the exotic Negro." In the "brute Negro" stereotype particularly, Brown tells us that both proslavery and abolitionist Whites painted Black people as savages, beastly, dangerous, and angry in literature. That characterization of Black people as angry has been sustained since Brown's investigation and today is one of the most prevailing stereotypes against Black people.

In Erica Wilkins et al.'s (2012) discussion of what clinicians and therapists should know about the residual effects of slavery, she offers true case vignettes of instances where Black youth may face the angry stereotype. As a matter of fact, even when Black people achieve the most admirable of accomplishments, ones that necessitate a restrained temperament, they are still stereotyped as angry. In 2012, then–First Lady Michelle Obama talked about how the stereotype was constantly and inaccurately used to describe her, saying, "That's been an image that people have tried to paint of me since the day Barack announced [he would run for president] — that I'm some angry black woman." In a candid interview with Oprah Winfrey, Michelle Obama discussed how the stereotype affected her, and she revealed that the stereotype does not fit her or most Black people, stating, "Well this isn't about me. This is about the person or the people who write it" (OWN, 2016).

The stereotype that Black people are angry is pervasive and overshadows Black people in virtually every facet of life, even if they reach the White House. Perhaps it does not need to be stated that this stereotype is false and racist, or perhaps it does need to be stated since the stereotype has existed since the 1800s. More concerning is that studies have proven the stereotype to be unfounded, which further validates the definition of Blackness presented earlier in this book. One notable example is Dr. J. Celeste Walley-Jean's (2009) study investigating the stereotype. Using well-established scales for measuring anger, Dr. Walley-Jean found that Black women actually report less anger compared to a normative sample of 977 women of different races and across a range of professions. What makes the findings of Dr. Walley-Jean more compelling is that Black women displayed less anger even when faced with criticism, disrespect, or negative evaluations. The work of Dr. Walley-Jean and others presents a conundrum because if there is evidence that the stereotype is not true, as is the case with most racial stereotypes imposed on Black people, then why has it existed for so long?

Distinguishing Racial Trauma from Hostile Anger

If we have empirical evidence that disproves the stereotype, why does it still exist? I affirm that aside from pure racial resentment — disdain for Black people — there is a benefit rooted in control as to why institutions and White people have held on to this stereotype. Referring back to the explanation of race by Dr. Lee Ann Bell (2016) in the chapter 1, we understand that race was created as a way to assign privileges and disadvantages. It was a means of control in which White culture, or Whiteness, controls other cultures. Thus, there remains a desire to control, and the angry stereotype allows control over two things: (1) White comfort and (2) the narrative of oppression experienced by Black people and other minorities.

The study of Adia Harvey Wingfield (2007) gives clear evidence that in public spaces, particularly places of employment, White people retain the angry Black stereotype to temper any Black voice or action that demands equity, as racial equity often encroaches on White people's moral self-image and makes them uncomfortable. Dr. Wingfield collected data from twenty-three Black college-educated professional men, ranging from lawyers to engineers. Her study revealed that White employers and supervisors intentionally applied the stereotype of "angry Black men" to Black men, despite occupational success or mannerisms, in the workforce as a method to pacify White comfort. All the Black men who had this stereotype applied to them had been what Cornel West calls *relatively conscious* — meaning they were aware of racism in many of the institutions and structures of their jobs, and as a result of calling it out, they were accused of being "enraged" (Wingfield, 2007, 205). Their calls for equitable changes made White coworkers and supervisors uncomfortable, and in an effort to reclaim the presumed White comfort, they labeled these professionals with impeccable credentials as angry as a way to dismiss their claims.

Connected to controlling their own comfort, the stereotype has been sustained in order to control the narrative of discrimination. LaMills Garrett, NAACP Criminal Justice and Political Action Chair, unapologetically explains this. He afforded that there is an aim in characterizing Black people as emotionally unstable persons, particularly angry, and that goal is to devalue the testimonies offered by Black people regarding their racialized experiences. Garrett stated that if what a Black person is saying "is viewed through more of a sense of emotion than from an outcome of fact," then there is a basis for rebutting or even dismissing the claim altogether. The "angry Black" stereotype, among other stereotypes and negative images, allowed and continues to allow White society to ignore the inequitable systemic realities experienced by Black people by reducing those claims to irrational rage (Walley-Jean, 2009). Such a seemingly simple falsehood dehumanizes the victims of racism by creating a "controlling image" that Black people do not have the ability to rationally articulate their condition while simultaneously exonerating the system, as an accusation is only the result of Black people's inability to be rational (Winfield, 2007, 201).

However, if Black people are not angrier than everyone else, why do even well-intentioned White people perceive Black responses as angry? Let us assume a White observer has no devious intention to use emotional projection as a tactic for dismissing Black experiences. Why would that person perceive a Black person as angry? I evoke that the White observer is seeing wide-ranging manifestations of racial trauma and confuses the traumatic responses with anger because White privilege exonerates them from the trauma in which they would have some experiential reference. In other words, they confuse racial trauma responses with hostile anger because their privilege exempts them from racial trauma.

It is important to delineate that trauma fundamentally differs from anger, as anger is rooted in hostility, according to the *Oxford English Dictionary*. Whereas, trauma, as explained by Eve Carlson (as cited by Robert Carter and Alex Pieterse [2020]), is an "emotionally painful (highly negative)" event, in which the target is faced with "sudden or unexpected" pain in a situation that is "uncontrollable." However, a person can exhibit anger in a situation in which they have control. Additionally, the response to the trauma of racism can cause a psychological affliction that is perceived as anger but, in reality, is distress. Furthermore, because "racial incidents are common and reoccurring in the lives of many people of color," White people are witnessing increased distress responses and deepened emotional pain, which, in their ignorance, they incorrectly classify as anger (Carter and Pieterse, 2020, 86).

The skeptic may inquire: How can I determine that the perceptions about Black people, rooted in the stereotype of anger, are actually racial trauma and not anger? Or, how can I determine any racial inaccuracy? I did the simple thing. I listened to other Black people. From December 2022 to November 2023, I conducted rigorous interviews of Black Americans with the sole purpose of understanding the anti-Black discriminatory nature of race and the products of that racism in the real lives of Black people. Through multiple interviews conducted under IRB protocol 1757, I talked to transgenerational Black Americans — Black Americans who have lived for multiple generations and in multiple racialized systems, as they were alive before the United States legalized racial segregation. I theorized that there would be no group better to facilitate to inquisition than the people who had experienced Blackness for multiple generations and lived in multiple legal racialized systems. What better way to ascertain the "Black experience" than to hear from Black Americans who have lived for multiple generations, across racial labels, and experience the legal and cultural shifts of race relations in America?

In this chapter, I specifically investigate those interviews to see if Black people are angry or suffering from entrenched racial trauma. The full collection of interviews revealed three themes that disprove the stereotype of the "angry Black" person, as they support Eve Carlson's characterization of trauma.

- Systemic racism is a stress-inflicted trauma. While this may seem like a "duh" moment, we must remember that some people do not even believe in the existence of systemic racism — the notion that both individuals and institutions operate in a way that perpetuates racial disadvantage. A 2022 *U.S. News & World Report-Harris Poll* found that 29 percent, almost one in every three, of White people do not believe that systemic racism exists. Thankfully, belief or disbelief is not a prerequisite for the truth. Still, Robert Carter and Alex Pieterse (2020) discuss extensively how systemic racism is a compounding stress from which White people are exempt. They say: "People of color in American society continue to experience social exclusion and rejection in ambiguous, unpredictable, and uncontrollable ways … the conditions of strain and deprivation that racism produces for many of its targets create a range of mental and physical health consequences … these experiences take place in addition to typical stressful life events" (Carter & Pieterse, 2020, 28).

• Anti-Black racism is experienced early in life, often in the developmental years. Racism, or being disadvantaged because of race, is not a singular event, as discussed in earlier chapters. It reoccurs over life spans. This informs us that Black citizens must develop "in" a racialized existence, and the existence is traumatic as it happens before cognitive defenses can be formed — unexpectedly. Additionally, this further reinforces the notion that racism produces trauma, as its continued recurrence shows that Black people have no control over the experiences the system assigns to them — one of the primary points Eve Carlson makes. Carter and Pieterse (2020) make this plain by saying, "Stress related to racial discrimination occurs over the life span, starting at birth … Blacks have the highest exposure and higher clustering of the stressors [throughout life]" (28).

• Emotional responses are common in response to stress and trauma. However, most Black Americans feel no hostility, and thus no anger, toward White people directly. If there is any anger, it is toward the systems that perpetuate anti-Black racism. The skeptic will likely be ready to note that in a 2020 Pew Research Survey, during the height of the racial protests, 81 percent of Black people affirmed they were angry about the murder of George Floyd. And, while I take no dispute with the statistic, what was the target of that anger, and was there hostility? The same Pew Research Survey confirms that Black people were not angry at White people but had "longstanding concerns about the treatment of Black people in the country" — 83 percent of Black citizens

> noting this as the cause. Again, Carter and Pieterse (2020) say, "If stress evokes anger, we may engage in negative or aggressive social behavior" (27). Yet between May 24, 2020, and August 20, 2024, the Armed Conflict Location and Event Data Project (ACLED) recorded more than 10,600 demonstration events across the country. "Over 10,100 of these — or nearly 95% — involve peaceful protesters. Fewer than 570 — or approximately 5% — involve demonstrators engaging in violence" (Kishi and Jones, 2020, para. 6).

These three themes were revealed in all interviews. However, this chapter focuses specifically on two interviewees: William Douglas Catching Jr. and Harriet Waters. These interviews are presented together because they convey that the disadvantageous nature of race in America is not regionally isolated.

Introducing William Douglas Catching Jr. (born in Pickens, Mississippi, on August 29, 1938)

Figure 3.1. William Douglas Catching Jr., interviewed on December 31, 2022. *Source*: Provided by the author. Used with permission.

William Catching was a very memorable interview because even at the age of eighty-four, which he was when the interview occurred, he had an impeccably sharp memory — remembering dates, times, places, facial expressions, and statements. He used those details to create a clear and indisputable narrative that he was not angry and had no hostility toward White people, but he had experienced a life of racial trauma that shaped how he viewed the world and how he operated as the patriarch of his family. He notes that, as with most, if not all, Black Americans, his first experience with racism was at an early age — five years old. He recounted this story.

> When I started school in 1943 [after my family had moved to St. Louis, Missouri], we went to a fully segregated school system. There were no White kids allowed to go to school with us, nor us to go with them. We were not allowed to go into any restaurants and sit down to eat. You could buy food, but you had to take it out. And they had certain areas in the city of St. Louis where we [as Black people] could live, no matter how much money you had …

He goes on to say,

> I traveled back and forth to Mississippi a lot in my younger [teen] years, and in our driving to and fro, we couldn't use the restrooms and service stations. We couldn't check into any hotel anywhere. We couldn't sit down and have a meal anywhere … Very seldom could you go into a service station and use the restroom. They [White people] would just straight out tell you "no," and you more or less had to stop in a Black neighborhood maybe and ask if you could use the restroom. We were on our way back, I remember very, very vividly in 1957, and we burned out a generator in the car — the brushes burned out in the generator. We had to spend a night in Memphis, and we had to find a Black family where we could stay overnight until we could have a car repaired the next morning and return to St. Louis because there were no hotel accommodations for us.

William was perhaps unaware that he gave an ideal illustration as to how the American system of race structurally works to disadvantage people who are not racialized as White, especially Black people. When William recounted the rules that prohibited Blacks from using restrooms, checking into hotels, or being served at restaurants, and the White people who would flat-out say "no" to Black requests, he was describing the structurally disadvantageous nature of race. The structurally disadvantageous nature of race refers to the interplay of institutions (societal organizations) that are based on a White notion of normal and individual actions that defend and sustain those institutions. I discuss institutions more in the next chapter. However, race fundamentally leads to disadvantages for some and advantages for others because race creates a structure where institutions and individuals are present, but both are not necessarily needed at the same time. If one could remove the racist individuals, they would still have to grapple with rules of institutions that often produce inequitable outcomes, and if they changed the rules, they would still have persons who accept and even desire the disadvantages race produces. The structure does not need both but uses both to "cyclically remanufacture racial inequity" (Harper, 2012, 10).

One would likely not question the early life experiences of Mr. Catching. However, those skeptical of its relevance may rebut that these incidents happened in the 1940s and 1950s. They would likely point to some indicators of "racial progress" to affirm that the country is in a better place or even go as far as to state that the country is postracial. Measures of racial progress in the United States are debatable; however, Dr. Harper's point should not be dismissed — the system of race evokes both an interplay of institutions and individuals within a structure to remanufacture unfairness. The negative and undesired outcomes of race are not isolated one-time incidents. They are recurring and perpetual. Thus, even if one could dismiss William's early life incidents, one could not dismiss the recurring experiences he endured throughout his lifetime, which he experienced solely because he is racialized as Black.

- In 1960, William recalled being mistreated by a White police officer and falsely charged with the suspicion of gambling in a pool hall that Mr. Catching never entered. "I was arrested, taken to jail; kept overnight for twenty-three hours … And didn't have that expunged until after I retired."
- In 1974, he was denied the right to purchase a house that he could afford in a more affluent neighborhood because he was a Black American.
- Toward the end of his employment at the Chrysler Plant in Fenton, Missouri, which officially closed in 1991, there still existed White superiority that would intentionally block individual attainment. "One of the [White] supervisors in Skilled Trades, he said, 'the only way that a Black person would get his skilled trades would be over his dead body.'"
- Presently, he discussed the reality of living in a majority White neighborhood where White neighbors have selectively segregated themselves from him and his family. "All of my neighbors are White … they still don't speak, but they speak to each other. Their kids play with other little White kids, but they won't play with my little great-grandkids, even though they're all out there at the cul-de-sac together."

And when asked how this lifetime of racial disadvantage had affected him, it was clear that he possessed the pain of trauma and not the hostility of anger.

In describing how racism impacted him, he used words such as *distant* and *skeptical*. However, there was no indication of hostility or anger, verbally or even nonverbally. Instead, he talked about the injury of racism, validating the trauma of racism. When asked about how this lifetime of racial experiences impacted him, he honestly answered: "You can say that you overlook them, but you really don't because it leaves a scar, a permanent scar. And the wounds are just too deep."

When asked directly, "What is your perception of White people currently?" Mr. Catching replied, "I trust up to a point." But skeptical mistrust isn't an emotional response associated with anger; it is often associated with trauma. I probed further and asked: What was that point to which he trusted White people? He simply replied, "The front door," meaning that he would not trust White people in his home. You see, for Mr. Catching, as for many Black Americans, society is so saturated with racism that their home is often the only place they believe the disadvantageous reach of race does not exist. Mr. Catching believed he had made his home a racism-free place, and for him, the only way to maintain that would be to keep those who have perpetrated the most egregious acts of racism out of his home. His acquired distrust of an entire race of people was indicative that he was not angry but reeled from racial trauma.

Introducing Harriet Vesey Waters (born in Wichita, Kansas, on January 7, 1946)

Figure 3.2. Harriet Vesey Waters, interviewed on May 11, 2023. *Source*: Provided by the author. Used with permission.

Harriet Waters is the second interview presented in this chapter. However, contrary to Mr. Catching, Harriet Waters notes that even though she likely experienced racism as a child, she was somewhat isolated from interpersonal racism because of racial segregation. Because she lived her youth in a Black community and could not interact with White people, she had no personal experience with anti-Black racism perpetrated by White people, even though the fact that she was segregated was because of racism. When asked to detail her first experience of interpersonal racism, she answered: "Let me preface that by saying it was no doubt always there, but I, as a child, wasn't subjected to it. I grew up in a Black community; went to an all-Black school. I didn't go to a largely integrated school until high school. So … it was really when I first started freshman/sophomore year in college that I first encountered really new 'slap in the face' [racism]."

Harriet notes her first experience with racism, in which she was conscious of the racism, took place well into her college years, and she detailed the experience as follows:

> I needed to work to help, you know, pay my way … there were three others still at home, still in school, and we didn't have a lot. So I wanted to do what I could, at least to work to get some spending money. So, I managed to get a job at the library there on campus … Kansas State College of Pittsburgh in Pittsburgh, Kansas. I got a job there, of course, evenings, working evenings. And I like that, you know, there wasn't much to do there at night. Students would come in and they were studying, you know, it wasn't noisy or anything like that. And, the supervisor and I, she was a Caucasian woman, we got along well. She was very nice. But she came to me one day, and she said that the Director of the library, an older Caucasian man, wanted her to let me go. And I said, "Well, why on earth? What have I done?" She said, "Well, he says you talked too much!" And I thought to myself, "This is a library. Who am I talking to?" I was just flabbergasted. That's what she said. "I talked too much!" And I was hurt really because I knew it wasn't true! And, you know, I was young. I couldn't have been more than 18 or 19. So I just let it go. I didn't go to him, I didn't confront him, you know, I had just lost that job.

Harriet's termination based on the lie that she was overly talkative reaffirms the definition of Blackness discussed in the previous chapter, specifically how false narratives lead to discriminatory and unfair outcomes. The director of the library, at best, had infrequent interactions with Harriet. Yet he was able to consciously craft a narrative about her that served as justification for terminating her. However, and often overlooked in discussions of race, are those who collude or support the unfair outcomes racialization produces by "going along," whether consciously or unconsciously (Bell et al., 2016, 138). Harriet's immediate supervisor is the real culprit in her unfair termination based on race. Her supervisor knew the justification was false because she stated, "He says you talked too much." She never agreed with such characterization and cognizantly distanced herself from the untrue accusation but was complicit in sustaining the prejudicial outcome. This White woman, whom Harriet spoke positively of, with whom she "got along well," seemingly fell in line with the falsehood because her own advantage and privilege as a White woman would not be diminished if Harriet no longer worked there, but she dare not leverage that privilege, even when she knew what was happening was wrong simply because of Harriet's race.

What I found impactful from interviewing Harriet is her discussions of how racism affected her, which she sprinkled throughout the interview. She repeatedly used words like *flabbergasted* and *hurt* to characterize her emotional responses to racism. However, she did use the word *anger*. In talking about an experience of being denied an apartment complex, she said, "It angered me." But it was not anger or hostility toward White people that is enveloped in the stereotype of Black people being angry. She articulated frustration with a system that relegated Black people to certain experiences. She did this by giving her version of the compounding effects of slavery and Jim Crow experienced by Black people. Now she may not have known that she was articulating the academic doctrines of the "residual effects of slavery and Jim Crow" discussed by Wilkins et al. (2012), but her articulation and illustration of a yarn ball evinces that her anger is not hostility but a resentment toward a racist system that has yet to treat Black people fairly.

> All of this stuff is like building a yarn ball, you know what I'm saying? A ball of yarn — you start out and you've got a little ball. People being captured and brought over here from Africa, the little ball grows. People being enslaved here, the yarn ball continues to grow. People being brutalized and not being able to continue to speak their own language. They're having to be renamed, take up other names, the ball continues to grow. Then, finally, slavery ends. But does it really in the minds of captures who had Black people enslaved? No, it doesn't. The yarn ball just continues to grow and grow, and then they're freed. And what does that mean, they're free? People who didn't have anything in the first place. You're all right, you're free? Well, you become sharecroppers and you're still just as much as if you were enslaved. So that yarn ball is still growing ... it doesn't matter. In the South, it was blatant, but in the North, it was more underhanded. Even though you have a segment of our society who don't want [fair] laws in effect, they come up with the excuses system. "Well that's, that's reverse discrimination." It's very difficult. ... Going back to the answer to your question,

> the effects of all of it has a bearing on today and it'll have a bearing on tomorrow because personally, how can we ever get out from under if we [Black people] continue to be slighted?

It was clear that a lifetime of racial trauma had impacted Harriet, just as it had William. However, toward the end of Harriet's interview, she discussed how the trauma impacted her as a woman of the Christian faith. She evoked that the racism of White people and White systems were contradictory to the messianic figure of Jesus that all Christians claim to serve. The injury of racism that never caused her to be hostile toward White people troubled her, but even religion couldn't seem to buffer against the saliency of American racism, specifically how Black Christians accommodated White Christians, which was rarely, if ever, reciprocated. This also injured her and she said.

> [White people] must think there's going to be a segregated heaven. Because I don't think, on the whole, I don't think they want to mingle with us, I really don't. And once in a great while, they'll have something that "well, come on over and join us in this praise session." You know, we go over there and sing and talk afterward, and you know what have-ya. But let us have something and invite them. You can hear the crickets. I mean, they don't come! They don't want you really to join, to become members of their congregation … to embrace one another when we're supposed to be Christ-like. But yet still we can't, we can't see Christ for seeing color.

Here, Harriet, perhaps unwittingly, captures the completeness of race because she noted that the visible difference, such as skin color, which racial systems use to assign advantage or disadvantage, brought about different experiences even for those of the same religion. Race as a social construct often determines human interaction regardless of the cultures, philosophies, and practices of other societal institutions. And, perhaps, that is what confused her the most. To borrow her own words, racism that is inherent to a system of race "flabbergasted" her!

Conclusion

Stereotypes are uninformed or overly simplified beliefs, perceptions, or attitudes imposed on an individual or group by those with privilege or power. The accuracy or truthfulness of the information used in the creation of stereotypes is rarely vetted, and even when evinced as false or biased, the group that perpetuates the stereotype(s) refuses to relinquish them. This explanation ideally describes the Black "angry" stereotype. It evolves from the untruthful, brutish characterization of Black slaves, and though anecdotes and academic research disprove that Black people are not inherently angry or hostile, the stereotype has endured for more than a century. Why? The answer is race. Race — the social concept to interpret and justify human differences — produced the stereotype under the racial dehumanization of slavery, and race, more accurately racial control, is the reason that White people have held on to the stereotype with the fiercest voracity. Painting Black people as angry or irate prevents any credible claim of inequity that would make White people uncomfortable and gives them control over the narrative or, rather, the narrative's validity.

Black people are not angry, but they do exist in constant race-based trauma. Race designates treatment to which the treatment endured by Black people is traumatizing, being beyond their control and stressful to their mental and physical health. Yet even given the trauma, Black people generally hold no hostility toward White people. The shared abbreviated life narratives of William Catching and Harriet Waters introduced in this chapter serve as affirmations that even with a lifetime of racism, they were more distrustful or confused than hostile and angry.

As we continue this reeducation about what it truly means to be racialized as Black, a proper reeducation must preemptively counter common narratives. It is likely that one may attempt to respond to this chapter and the real lived experiences included by stating that the experiences of racial trauma are because of individuals rather than an indictment of the entire concept of race. However, institutions are culpable in the mistreatment of Black people. The next chapter begins with this affirmation from the famed author and activist James Baldwin. To substantiate this point, the chapter does a comprehensive case study of policing as an institution to demonstrate that institutions were designed, sustained, and cultivated to respond differently to Black citizens. To show that this premise extends beyond the institution of the police, the chapter introduces another life narrative from the collection of Black interviews. This interview further shows how other institutions are implicated in racial mistreatment. The next chapter poses the question: "Do you know that the institutions that serve you destroy us?"

Chapter 4

"Do You Know that the Institutions that Serve You Destroy Us?"

"I don't know what most White people in this country feel. But, I can only conclude what they feel from that state of their institutions." This is one of the most famous quotes from writer and civil rights activist James Baldwin, but the teachability of this statement is made more valuable when understanding the context in which Baldwin made this statement. Baldwin was a guest on the *Dick Cavett Show* in May of 1969, invited on the show to discuss race. Halfway through Cavett's interview with Baldwin, he included Professor Paul Weiss — a professor of philosophy at Yale University who happened to be White. Now, according to the standards of education, Weiss was superior to Baldwin and positioned himself in opposition to Baldwin, not only in terms of his posture but also in his postulation. It was evident that Weiss was added as a guest to counter the racial arguments made by Baldwin. It was clear that what was once an interview was now a debate, and Professor Weiss believed himself to be winning based on the audience's applauses. A particularly poignant point was when Professor Weiss affirmed Baldwin's success as an author to refute Baldwin's claim that Black people were oppressed. Baldwin responded by informing Weiss that he had to leave the US and travel to France to escape a "social terror," which made it possible for him to come into his own as an author. When Weiss inferred that Baldwin's general language about the oppressive nature of race was painting every White person as a terror to Black people, it was then that Baldwin responded with: "I don't know what most White people in this country feel. But, I can only include what they feel from that state of their institutions."

This response from Baldwin adds to the reeducation discussed in this book, because even after the legislative successes of the African American Civil Rights Movement, he reaffirmed that the disadvantageous nature of race involves more than negative interpersonal interactions with people. Baldwin educated Professor Weiss by letting him and the audience know that the disadvantages assigned under race are reflected in institutions. Baldwin went on to say the following:

> I don't know if White Christians hate Negroes or not, but I know we have a Christian church which is White and a Christian church which is Black ... I don't know whether the labor unions

> and their bosses really hate me. That doesn't matter, but I know I'm not in their unions. I don't know if the Real Estate Lobby has anything against Black people, but I know the Real Estate Lobby is keeping me in the ghetto. I don't know if the board of education hates Black people, but I know the textbooks they give my children to read and the schools that we have to go to.

Baldwin articulated that the inequitable racial outcomes we often witness in reports and in media are not necessarily because of individual actions but because institutions operate racially. He affirms that the institutions that White people rely on daily simultaneously oppress and, in some cases, destroy Black people. By delineating this, he teaches that the oppressive nature of race has less to do with whether individual White people or people of any race dislike Black people. It is more about how oppression is institutionalized — the organizations of society cause, sustain, and, in some cases, defend the inequitable outcomes that occur racially. Simultaneously, these institutions protect and preserve White citizens. This is another experiential component of race because one racial group experiences the institution positively and with an air of service, while the same institution degrades and destroys another race.

However, understanding that there are those who would be skeptical and resistant to the notion that an institution, organization, or association produces racial outcomes that benefit some races while marginalizing and even destroying others. It is necessary to simply demonstrate the differing racial outcomes Baldwin spoke of by looking at the institutions this country seemingly relies on. But where to begin? I believe that the answer is obvious — the police. Policing is an institution in the US, and consistently across every database, there are racial differences in opinions about fairness and trust regarding policing.

- The American National Election Study, 2016, as referenced by Lewis and Nelson (2022), informs that 85 percent of Black Americans believe that White people are treated better by the police.
- Pew Research (2022) notes that race and ethnicity are the areas where there is the greatest difference regarding police. Only 10 percent of Black Americans have a great deal of confidence in the police.
- A 2024 Axios article notes that 82 percent of Black Americans believe that Black people are incarcerated at higher rates than White Americans — a fact that is supported by the US Department of Justice's 2022 Prisoner's Summary.

Are these opinion statistics reliable? Some would argue that these statistics are simple opinions and not reliable. To substantiate the fact that institutions produce different treatments for races, I employ a historical case study of the police. This is not intended to be antipolice, but as an institution, the police has one of the most enduring histories in this country and, in many ways, is reflective of societal thought regarding race, making it an ideal institution to investigate.

A Case Study of Policing in the US

"Look, if you hate cops just because they're cops, the next time you're in trouble, call a crackhead." One would think such a statement was awfully delivered humor from an uninformed shock-jock, but this phrase is from a televised ad of a White US senator seeking reelection in the 2022 midterm. Senator John Kennedy (R) of Louisiana ended a television ad with that phrase to attack those who supported the political movement, "Defund the Police." Defund the Police is a movement that gained political and social attention during the 2020 racial protests in response to the killings of Ahmaud Arbery, Breanna Taylor, and George Floyd. It is a policy proposal and a movement that demands "a shift in public budgeting policies … This movement asks not to eradicate policing agencies, but instead for more equitable budgeting policies by reallocating public resources from police departments to other local government and community agencies to support community safety and wellness" (Gaynor et al., 2021, 63).

However, many White people such as Senator Kennedy fail to see the logic in defunding an institution whose motto is "Protect and serve." Similar to Senator Kennedy, these people often disrespectfully mock persons who do not see the police as the inclusive executors of justice. I surmise that this is because how you are racialized determines your experiences with the respective institution, and this is evidently true with policing. Being White produces a privileged interaction with the institution that leaves no reason to question the legitimacy of the police motto. This is true even when the crimes committed by White people are particularly savage, such as mass shootings. Almost all mass shooters are White (Statista, 2022), and they are almost always captured alive by police and even treated to Burger King, as was in the case of Dylann Roof. Yet according to the peer-reviewed research by Frank Edwards, Hedwig Lee, and Michael Esposito (2019), published in the *Proceedings of the National Academy of Sciences*, police use of force is a leading cause of death for Black people. "Black men are about 2.5 times more likely to be killed by police over the life course than are White men. Black women are about 1.4 times more likely to be killed by police than are White women" (Edwards et al., 2019, para. 11). What is more alarming about the Edwards et al. (2019) study is that one cannot age out of the destructive nature of race perpetuated by the institution of policing, as the scholars state that "inequalities in risk persist throughout the life course" (para. 15). In short, each race has a different perspective because race assigns different experiences with the police and likely every societal institution. How are drastic inequitable outcomes evidenced in the institution of the police? What people often are unaware of, or rather what they often dismiss, is that institutions are created with racial considerations, and policing is no exception. The institution of law enforcement, as with most institutions, was created with racial consideration in mind.

Many White people, and maybe a portion of Black Americans, are nescient of the history of the police — a history that, when factually shared, informs us that the police, as an institution, was created for a racist purpose and sustained because of how efficient it was at producing those racially unfair outcomes. Let's begin with the historical fact that the US did not always have police. In the infancy of this nation, there existed two systems of enforcement: the Night Watch and the Slave Patrol. The Night Watch, created in 1631 in Boston, Massachusetts, was a patrol that operated by night but had no real power to arrest White colonists or enforce laws. As a matter of fact, the "watchmen," as they were called, did nothing more than drink at night under the presumption that White colonists were inherently moral and good people with no need for oversight. However, in 1704, the Carolina colonies created something called the Slave Patrol because, in contrast to perceptions of White morality, White people perceived slaves as savages who needed to be controlled with a "high level of brutality and ruthlessness" because Black people were inherently immoral (Archbold, 2012, 5). Thus, there were two systems of enforcement: (1) the Night Watch of lax enforcement because White people perceived themselves as inherently moral and (2) the Slave Patrol because of the slave's inherent savagery that needed legal enforcement.

But something happened in 1829, noted by the Boston Museum of African American History run by the National Park Service/US Department of Interior — a Black abolitionist in Boston, Massachusetts, named David Walker published *An Appeal to the Coloured Citizens of the World*, calling for a violent rebellion against the system of slavery. Walker was never a slave, as he was born in a free state. In his manuscript, Walker stated something that forever changed the US, and led to the creation of the modern police force. In his publication, he stated, "One good Black man can put to death six White men." It was Walker's call for a nationwide slave revolt, and needless to say, David Walker was found dead within the year. But the US, especially the Northeast, was forever changed, as in response to Walker's words, there were a series of attacks and violent exchanges between abolitionists and overt racists, which included an attempt to lynch William Lloyd Garrison. Walker's words and the subsequent chaos spread from Boston to terrified Southern slave owners, as at this time, there were more than two million slaves in the South, and the number was growing. In direct response to White fear over the concept of free, unrestrained, and savage Black people, Boston created the first full-time police force in 1838, with the sole intention of protecting White people and White property from a possible insurrection of Black abolitionists and escaped slaves.

Boston then served as the model for all subsequent police forces — an official unit to protect Whiteness while being threatening to Blackness — New York City in 1845, St. Louis in 1846, Chicago in 1854, and Los Angeles in 1869 (Archbold, 2012, 5). Thus, the roots of policing in the US were not to "protect and serve" all people but to protect White people and property from

Black people. The use of race in the invention of the police was that White lives and White property were protected while Black lives were expendable. My question to you, the reader, is: If differing treatment on the basis of race was the reason policing was created, when was that dynamic changed? What piece of national legislation, major cultural upheaval, or monumental uprising took considerations of race from the institutions of the police? The answer is none, and the distinct treatment by the institution has endured.

Even after the Civil War, policing was highly racialized primarily because it was determined by extreme politicization. There were "virtually no standards for hiring or training police officers" (Archbold, 2012, 7). Systemically, policing lacked structure, and this allowed local municipalities across the nation to turn Slave Patrols into the police (Reichel, 1988). This means that the same dehumanization, violence, and racial bigotry that governed the Slave Patrol now regulated every aspect of the Police, and this was not limited to the South as Jim Crow was a national racial culture. "Local municipalities leaned on police to enforce and exert excessive brutality on African Americans who violated any Jim Crow law" (NAACP, 2024). From that point until the present, policing as a practice of the institution has been to enforce the law disproportionately against Black people and often employ an excessive use of force and brutality. To note this in a more nuanced way, I want to return to the interview of William Catching, introduced in the previous chapter, as his narrative articulates this most compellingly.

> When I grew up in the neighborhood that I grew up in, there were two young men killed by police officers — White police officers. One was running from the police officer, but yet he was shot in the front of the head. How do you explain that? The other was running from the police officer, gunned down in broad daylight. Thirty-one or thirty-two people saw it, witnessed it, and they said there wasn't enough evidence to convict the White officer. A friend of mine, we had just parted for the evening to go home. He went in a restaurant and bought some barbecue. [He] came out and walked a little less than a half a block. He met a walking police officer. I went the other way, going home, and the police officer stopped him, asked him no, not ask him, told him to throw away his barbecue plate. And he said, "Well, this is this is my dinner. This is all I have. I'm on my way home." He said, "I said throw it into the trash can." He didn't throw it in the trash can quick enough, and the police officer hit him right up under the eye with a nightstick. Knocked him completely out ... These things coming up as a young man that we witnessed in our neighborhood, almost on a regular basis of being mistreated by White police officers, gives you a very dim view of them. When you see on their car the saying, "To protect and to serve." That didn't mean us! They were here to protect and to serve White people, not Black people.

In every dispensation of the American experiment, the police, as an institution, has treated citizens differently on the basis of race, notably the harassment, dehumanization, assault, and state-sanction killing of Black people. This is why conversations that employ the platitude of "a few bad apples" frustrate Black people. Those who use the phrase are seeing the police as a conglomerate of individuals who are primarily reasonable, law-abiding enforcers of justice infiltrated by a few morally corrupt persons. However, when most Black people have conversations about racial mistreatment in policing, they are referring to an institution, an association that was founded on the premise of treating people differently because of race, and it is so efficient at doing Black destruction, which it has done since its inception, it is now the accepted norm.

Policing Is One Institution, What About Others?

The premise that race is about differing treatment from institutions is not limited to the police but is true with most major US institutions. For example, health care is an institution with a long history of differing treatment for Black people, from the horrors of the Tuskegee Syphilis Study to the disproportionate treatment of Black people during the COVID pandemic, where in 2020, Black Americans were disproportionately making up the largest ratio of COVID deaths and the lack of access to testing (Reyes, 2020). This mistreatment in health care is institutionalized, as unfounded racial myths are taught in colleges and universities as health care facts. The widely used textbook *Nursing: A Concept-Based Approach to Learning* teaches nursing students not to believe Black women when they report pain because "They believe suffering and pain are inevitable." This may be directly linked to complications in labor and high infant mortality rates. According to the Centers for Disease Control, Black women had the highest neonatal rates in 2021, almost three times that of White women (Ely and Driscoll, 2023). Similar to policing, health care, as an institution, imposes differing treatment on Black people that, in many cases, ends in a loss of life.

However, we can move beyond health care to banking and finance. Banks and other credit institutions have engaged in discriminatory practices since Reconstruction. According to historian Frank Toland, not only did the Black Codes — legislative attempts to limit any notion of citizenship newly freed Blacks could exercise — prevent Black people from voting, but they also institutionalized discriminatory practices that prevented Black people from getting mortgages and loans. Likely the most common discriminatory practice in the pursuit of home ownership is redlining. Redlining is a practice by the government and financial institutions that officially designates Black residential areas as risky investments, leading to the denial of mortgages, preventing investment, and encouraging divestment (Jackson, 2021). The practices continued and became one of the primary issues of the African American Civil Rights

Movement, as banks overt discriminatory practices to prevent Black purchase of homes or even improve existing home infrastructure integrity for those who had homes (Taibi, 1994). As Anthony Taibi writes in the *Harvard Law Review*, these practices, specifically mortgage discrimination, may be beyond the grasp of anyone to fully comprehend because the discrimination of banks is so accepted that it discourages Black people from applying for loans when they are treated differently in the preapproval process or when they face loan officers with biases (1994, 1475).

One may ask: How does being denied a home destroy Black lives? These practices by banks are rooted in the perception that Black neighborhoods are high risk and the resulting divestment from redlining and other practices make the appearance of Black neighborhoods seem less safe; and, according to research published in the *American Journal of Public Health*, when these communities appear less safe, this causes delays in medical care responsiveness — the time it takes for medical emergency services, such as EMTs, to respond (Ortiz and Zimmerman, 2012). Even more damning are the benefits that homeownership bestows to White residents that Black citizens simply cannot enjoy, as discriminatory practices often keep them from owning homes. For White people who own homes, they are less likely to be prevented from even the most basic of health care needs, such as obtaining a prescription (Ortiz and Zimmerman, 2012). Homeownership has an impact on the timeliness of emergency medical responsiveness and a direct response to prescription needs, and both can be life or death issues.

These differing experiences for races in banking are worse when moving beyond mortgages and ventures into small business pursuits. "[When] Black and White business owners [have] identical predictive traits — age, educational background, a close family member who is a business owner or self-employed professional, purchase of an ongoing concern, and position of equity capital — [Black people] do not receive equal treatment" (Taibi, 1994, 1476). According to the US Small Business Administration's 7(a) and 504 Report, used by *Forbes*, as of 2023, White people account for 42 percent of all small business–approved loans totaling more than ten million, whereas Black people only account for 7 percent.

For most institutions, racialized treatment was present in the origination of the institution, and current outcomes demonstrate a sustained racial dynamic with White protection and Black endangerment. As the definition of Black presented in a previous chapter informs, it is a sociopolitical identity rooted in discrimination and disadvantage, and societal institutions make this discrimination life-altering and, in some instances, life-ending. However, as this book is a reeducation from the perspective of Black people, it would be prudent to preempt skeptics by turning toward the real lived experiences of transgenerational Black Americans. The upcoming interview reinforces the central premise in this chapter with compelling accounts of institutional discrimination and does so by looking at other institutions.

Introducing Jacqueline Barnes-Simmons (born in Martin, Tennessee, on September 10, 1945)

Figure 4.1. Jacqueline Barnes-Simmons, interviewed March 2, 2023. *Source*: Provided by the author. Used with permission.

The interview with Ms. Simmons was one for the history books, which is not surprising as she is unofficially known as "the historian" for those who are a part of the Church of Christ Christian faith in the greater St. Louis area. In her unofficial capacity as a historian, she has an uncanny ability to unbiasedly recount events that seemingly transport the listener back in time. And this ability was on full display as she recounted her life experiences. In our interview, similar to the interview of William Catching, you will read how racial disadvantage was made apparent early in life. And similar to the interview with Harriet Waters, you will read how the disadvantages inherent to race were recurring and largely beyond the control of Black victims. However, Jacqueline's interview, without prompt, seemed laser-focused to show how the racial mistreatment Black people faced was not primarily because of interpersonal racism but because institutions embodied differential treatment based on race.

Ms. Simmons notes that her first experience where her race made it apparent that she would be treated differently was when she was around seven years old.

> When we moved to St. Louis, we used to go travel every year to Tennessee to see my grandparents. And when traveling, Blacks weren't allowed, you couldn't stop like at the restrooms, or you couldn't stop in places to eat or anything like that. So, you had to pack your lunches and everything; and then to use the restroom, you had to stop on the side of the road because you weren't allowed to go to the restrooms. You could buy gas, but you couldn't use the restrooms.

She goes on to explain the forced ingenuity of Black people in the face of racism, noting that her family came up with their own way to attempt privacy amid the humiliation of having to use the restroom on the side of the road. She says, "You would open the back door and the front door [to serve as a stall] so people that were driving by couldn't see, you know, couldn't see you using the restroom." And, even in her youth, the contempt that being Black imposed on her never prompted anger. In the case of Ms. Simmons, it prompted consciousness of acceptance. She says, "There was no really, I guess, hatred or anything. At that point in time, you just knew that you were Black and they were White. And they had certain rights, and you didn't have certain rights."

However, it was when Jacqueline was asked about her most traumatizing experience of racism that it became clear she understood how institutions reinforced racial mistreatment. For her, the most traumatizing experience with racism was an indictment on the institution of higher education. When she, as many do, left home to pursue a college degree, she encountered an experience with racism where the university, as an institution, traumatized her so severely that she never completed her college education.

> It was in August of 1963. My cousin convinced me they were trying to get Blacks to enter the University of Tennessee — Martin Branch. And she was saying, "You need to come down here and go to school with me." And so [my mother] agreed. Her and my father agreed because my grandmother was there ... So, at that time, it was like seven of us (Black students admitted). It was five young ladies and two young men. We were the first Blacks to enter the University of Tennessee in Martin at that time ... You would get to the class; you'd be the only [Black person] in the classroom, the only one in the class ... as soon as you walked out of the door on campus, you would be called "nigger" and told to "go home!" So, at lunchtime, we had to walk all the way back to the Black school to eat lunch because we weren't allowed to eat at the college ... every day ... We'd have class; we would walk all the way back to the Black school, which was K–12 at that time, and eat lunch. And then we walk all the way back. And the Principal, Mr. Connors, he would tell us, we were told not to say anything, not to talk back, regardless of what they called us ... "Just ignore it. Don't do anything,"

> which was really hard — somebody called you "Black" and "nigger" and all of this kind of stuff … I couldn't deal with it. So, I came back home [to St. Louis]. I just couldn't deal with that … It was just trauma because it was hard, you know. No matter what you did, you still got you didn't get above the "C" … you know, that was the grade for Black folks … no matter how smart you were … I think out of the seven, four stayed and graduated, and the other three went elsewhere … I went and found a job.

One may falsely think that Jacqueline's experience could be pinpointed to the persons shouting racial epithets or to the teachers who refused to grade fairly. But Ms. Simmons's racial mistreatment cannot be blamed on individuals who, against campus culture, college policies, or educational norms, mistreated her. Her differing treatment of being called a "nigger" every time she walked through campus was because the campus culture allowed and likely promoted it. There was no one stepping forward to rebuke those who used the slur, or there were no calls for greater inclusion of these seven Black students, of whom Jacqueline was a part. The discrimination existed because the institution assigned a degrading treatment to the Black students and an affirming type of treatment to the White students. When Ms. Simmons and her peers could not eat in the cafeteria of a school they were officially enrolled in, having to travel across town on foot to the Black K–12 school nine years after *Brown v. Board of Education*, it was because the policies of the university prohibited their presence in certain spaces. The rules, whether explicitly written or covertly disguised, assigned a degrading and inconvenient treatment to the Black students while comfort and access to the White students. And when no matter the course, professor, or quality of student work, the Black student could only earn the grade of C, it was because it was deemed the norm that Black students were intellectually inferior and could not excel in academics.

Jacqueline's life experiences indicted a plethora of institutions, but most notably, she, in her own ways, indicted the entire system of American capitalism. Capitalism is a system of economic activity where the economic industry is controlled by individual private owners who act in ways that they think would best benefit them (Krutz, 2021, 8). But even capitalism has inferred different experiences on Black people. In Dr. Sherice Nelson's book, *The Congressional Black Caucus: Fifty Years of Fighting for Equality*, she writes, "In a capitalistic country, Blacks are too often denied opportunities to [simply] work" — an issue the Congressional Black Caucus has attempted to address since its creation (2021, 97). Mrs. Simmons says, "I applied for jobs I knew I could do, and I didn't get them. And I knew I didn't get them because I was Black. And I could have done the job twenty times better than the person that got the job, but I didn't get the job because I was Black. So they kinda held you in certain positions."

Jacqueline's words are deeply damning of capitalism because racism had already taught her not to invest her time and energy in endeavors where she knew her race would be a barrier for her. However, even when she believed her credentials should have trumped the disadvantages of racism — that her employment would produce the greatest benefit for the owners — she was sadly mistaken, as Black people were denied the dignity of work, even when they were more qualified. Even capitalism conferred a different experience to Black citizens compared to White ones.

Conclusion

James Baldwin shifts accusations of racial mistreatment away from individual actors and indicts institutions. Therein lies the brilliance of Baldwin because he did not attempt to point to the consciousness of White individuals in order to evince racism, even when challenged by his own achievements. He knew that discussions of race often evoke White defenses and angst, or what Kendra King (2010) calls "knee-jerk reactions." He, on the other hand, elucidated that there are institutions whose racialized outcomes evince the oppression and mistreatment of Black people. He indicted the Christian faith, labor unions, and real estate as the consistent and long-term race-disaggregated data cannot be denied. Even more brilliant, since most of these institutions were created and are controlled by White people and embody White norms, if White people want exoneration from any accusation of racism, then they must correct the institutions they control, or they cannot hold on to their moral self-views.

Building on Baldwin's assertion, the case study in this chapter demonstrates how policing as an institution confers different treatment based on race. The notion of treating race differently was in the police's founding, specifically created to protect White people and White-owned property from the presumed evil of Black people. The institution's view of Black people as dangerous has been sustained, if not embraced, which is why police use of force is presently a leading cause of death for Black citizens. As stated before, in every dispensation of the American experiment, the police, as an institution, has treated citizens differently on the basis of race, notably the harassment, dehumanization, assault, and state-sanction killing of Black people. But it isn't just the police; health care and banking also destroy some aspects of Black lives. If the evidence from these institutions was insufficient, then the narratives of Jacqueline Simmons show how higher education and capitalism are also institutions that support racism.

What is the common thread across these narratives? The traditions, norms, policies, and cultures of organizations created and even cultivated the oppression of Black people. These same institutions protected and affirmed White people. But is there any point in the life of a Black citizen where race does not impose a discriminatory treatment? Perhaps some stage of life where institutions are less discriminatory to Black people. In the next chapter, we explore this under the posed question: Do you know Black youth are robbed of healthy childhoods?

Chapter 5

"Do You Know Black Youth Are Robbed of Healthy Childhoods?"

> This case demonstrates a severe instance in which a Black youth was seen as criminal, absent evidence. It typifies the historical stigmatization and normalization of young Black men in a negative light.
>
> — Allen and Metcalf, *Historicizing Fear*

This quote is from the book *Historicizing Fear*. In this book, Quaylan Allen and Henry Metcalf (2020) write a chapter on the fear of Black men in the US. But the above quote does not reference a man, or at least a male of legal age to be considered an adult. The quote references the account of George Stinney, who, by every measure, was a child. For those who are unfamiliar with the situation, George Stinney was a Black teenager and the youngest person legally executed in the US, based on a judicial sentence of capital punishment. At only fourteen years old, Stinney was electrocuted on June 16, 1944.

The facts of the case were, and perhaps still are, reflective of the reality of non-White people in the criminal justice system. According to Standford University, Stinney was questioned absent his parents and was claimed to have confessed, but there was never a written or signed statement. To add insult to injury, Stinney was represented by a tax attorney who had never argued a criminal case and had no intent of trying to defend Stinney, noted by the fact that he refused to call a single witness. The entire trial lasted less than three hours, prompting the all-White jury to find George guilty in ten minutes. With all certainty, George Stinney was killed simply because he was Black, and his age, an age of innocence and carefree exploration of the world, had no mitigating effect on the fact that society had deemed his life dispensable because he was Black.

To be clear, this book does not claim that Stinney was killed solely because of interpersonal racism. Yes, many White people in Columbia, South Carolina, in 1944 likely possessed racial animus, but Stinney was killed because of his race — he was Black. Being racialized as Black had imposed a life sentence on him despite whether or not the White people involved had some form of conscious racism. Being Black, even at the age of fourteen, robbed the adolescent of any presumption of innocence or any legitimate claim to due process, and being Black automatically made the ninety-pound teen a threat that had to be eliminated.

Allen and Metcalf (2020) would agree, as their book chapter says, that the tragedy of George Stinney portrays another aspect of race, and that is the criminalization of Black youth, especially Black boys, and that such is normal in the United States. According to Allen and Metcalf, Stinney, though still a youth, was a threat to White girls, and therefore, "his execution could be interpreted as White men protecting the White female body" from a Black body (2020, 22). And the age or maturity of the Black body was irrelevant because being Black predetermines danger despite age. Essentially, being racialized as Black automatically created then, and still creates, an irrational fear for White people. As the killing of George Stinney shows, the fear of Black people is so engrained in White thought that even the supposed innocence of childhood does not nullify the apparent danger that is inherent to being Black.

In childhood, most Black people cannot experience the carefree virtue assigned to White kids that allows the freedom of mistakes and learning from those mistakes. On the contrary, Black youth are not treated as adolescents even in their development years, because race imposes a reality on them whereby they are not children, only threats. This assertion is more than overzealous postulation. The peer-reviewed research of Phillip Goff et al. (2014) proved this. These scholars conducted a study at a large public university of a mostly female, mostly White group of collegiate students, where the median age of participants was nineteen years old. The researchers inquired about the perceived innocence of Black children, White children, and children generally. By comparing perceptions of innocence among a White sample of the population, Black children were perceived as "significantly less innocent" than White children (Goff et al., 2014, 529). Guilt, mischievousness, and any other designation that is the opposite of innocent is how society sees Black children. Simply by being racialized as Black, and Black alone, youth are robbed of blamelessness. The racialized society literally steals what is innately given to other youth — reasonable expectations of childhood innocence and healthy early life development. But is the case of George Stinney a single example that has been maligned for the purpose of a narrative, or is it an indictment of race in American society?

How Does Being Racialized as Black Rob Black Youth?

It is prudent to remind ourselves that racialized systems categorize people differently for a reason. As has been clearly shown in previous chapters, the categorization bestows certain privileges to some while denying those privileges to others. However, some privileges are innately given. One such privilege is that all humans are born equal — meaning they merit the same inherent humanizing dignity in how they are treated by the society in which they are born. However, if that society, because of race, takes that humanizing treatment or takes their life without cause, then that society uses race as a justification to steal. This chapter makes the claim that being racialized as Black robs even Black youth of the inherent humanizing dignity necessary for a healthy childhood.

The system of race robs Black youth of healthy childhoods in at least two simple ways. First, as with George Stinney, it robs them of life altogether. Understandably, the skeptic may accuse this writer of cherry-picking a blight from the past in the case of George Stinney. However, the plethora of current examples counter such ignorance. Black youth, especially Black boys, are often killed simply for existing in ways that White boys do. One could point to the killing of Trayvon Martin on February 26, 2012, by George Zimmerman. Zimmerman, who identifies as a White Hispanic, deemed Martin's race and his hoodie so great a threat that he called 9-1-1 to report a "suspicious person" and then confronted Martin against the directions of the dispatcher, carrying a pistol that he would eventually use to kill the seventeen-year-old youth. Two years after Trayvon Martin was murdered, Tamir Rice, a Black boy several years younger than Martin, was killed in a park while playing with a toy gun — an activity that most boys do, including this author when he was a boy. Rice was only twelve years old when a police officer shot him on November 22, 2014. But, it was not the toy gun that made Rice a threat. It was, however, the fact that he was never perceived as a child playing with a common child's toy because he was Black. According to the abbreviated detailing by Rebecca Wanzo (2015), the police officer who shot Rice within seconds of driving up to him identified him as a "Black male, maybe 20." Four years after Rice, police killed seventeen-year-old Antwon Rose Jr., who was perceived as so great a threat that he was shot in the back while fleeing an incident that he may have been involved in, though he had no weapon and was never given a directive from officers. These are only a few examples among many that demonstrate how being Black is sufficient cause to rob Black youth of their lives, as their race removes the shield of innocent harmlessness that most youth enjoy.

If Black youth manage to survive the imminent dangers of a society seeking to rob them of life, then they are under the shroud of constantly being seen as unintellectual imbeciles and/or often immoral malefactors. This means that if society does not kill them outright, it seeks to kill their capabilities, virtues, or any other thing that makes them human, and this is the second way being Black robs Black youth. Society dehumanizes them! To see examples of this dehumanizing characterization imposed on Black youth, just take a look at the origins of Black children's literature. According to Violet Harris (1990), "children's literature regarding African Americans has been replete with stereotypes" (541). In literature, historically, Black youth were "depicted as dim-witted children who constantly grin, eat, misunderstand simple directions, and scratch their heads" (Harris, 1990, 542). One classic example is *Little Black Sambo*, published over a century ago in 1899. The story tells of a Tamil boy's encounter with tigers in which he exchanges his colorful new clothes with the tigers to avoid being eaten. Vanity leads the tigers to their demise, and Sambo, his father, and his mother end the story with a feast of pancakes. And while the story seems innocent in its simplistic plot, the grotesque illustrations and mocking language are clearly rooted in a dehumanizing view of Black people, so much so that the National Museum of African American History and Culture categorizes the book under "Racist and Stereotypical Objects."

Beyond insults of Black youths' intelligence, a more perilous aspect of race is the notion of Black youth being automatically seen as immoral. The way Black youth are robbed of assumptions of innocence and automatically seen as needing greater discipline is evinced by school disciplinary rates. The commonly referenced study of Kimberlé Crenshaw, *Black Girls Matter: Pushed Out, Overpoliced and Underprotected*, provides evidence of the disparity for Black girls particularly. "The suspension and expulsion rates for Black girls far outpace the rates for other girls — and in some places, they outpace the rates of most boys" (Crenshaw, 14). Black girls are often labeled as loud, rebellious troublemakers who incite classroom environments toward unruliness. As a result, they are suspended at six times the rate of White girls. I can anticipate the rebuttal that falsely affirms that perhaps Black girls are indeed misbehaving more than others. However, according to a 2018 special issue on the "School to Prison Pipeline" in the *Journal of Culture and Education*, Black students do not misbehave at a rate higher than White students. However, they are placed in a school culture of "targeted control" (15). According to Crenshaw, this targeted control is the culture and practice that Black children need discipline over education because of the accepted notion that they lack morality. "They are perceived to be unruly, loud, and unmanageable," and schoolteachers, administrators, and safety personnel issue discipline not on the basis of actions but on the perceptions of disruptions (Crenshaw, 24).

Because of this racial theft, Black children live their lives in survival mode, as the system sees them as something meriting termination, and if they can avoid termination, they live under the dehumanizing shroud of being less innocent than their White peers, mandating discipline. However, there are other obscure, perhaps indirect ways in which being racialized as Black robs Black children of healthy childhoods. To explore this, we introduce another interviewee from the collected interviews of transgenerational Black Americans.

Introducing Irma Jean Wasp Lewis (born in Point Clear, Alabama, on July 25, 1945)

Though all of the interviewees talked about early life experiences where their race informed them that they were assigned different societal treatment, the interview with Mrs. Lewis evinced the notion in this chapter almost flawlessly. Not only does her real lived experiences show how Black youth are literally in survival mode because being Black deems young lives dispensable, but her life experiences add and contribute to the ways in which being racialized as Black steals from Black children. By her own volition, Irma discussed early life experiences more than all interview participants, even though she was interviewed from the same set of interview questions.

When asked about her earliest experience where her race was made apparent to her, Irma discussed an episode of clear reprehensible racism that occurred when she was only ten years old. It was an experience where the vitriolic danger often faced by Black youth was in no way tempered by children's innocence. She detailed the following:

> It was one night. I think I was about I was about ten, ten years old. Some Ku Klux Klans rode up to the house, and they were on horses, but they had it with the white hoods on. And my daddy, he didn't have, but one little gun and it was up over the door. And he was pushing us back because we were trying to look out the window to see what was going on. And he was so scared and he just kept pushing us back. He wouldn't let us come to the window so we could look out. And they burned that cross there in front of the door in front of the house. And when the cross went out, they took off on their horses, and they went up the Marlo Road from the house.

Figure 5.1. Irma Jean Wasp Lewis, interviewed on May 20, 2023. *Source*: Provided by the author. Used with permission.

Though the Klan's act of burning crosses was not a new or unheard-of intimidation tactic, it is particularly poignant here because the KKK could not claim ignorance, as the Wasp family had resided on the land for at least two decades and was a large family — the Klan knew there were children in the Wasp homestead. However, the Klan's scare tactics, likely to antagonize some actions where they could commit violence, had no regard for innocence in that home. Though she and her siblings naively tried to see the spectacle of the burning cross, they had no idea of the probable danger they were in, as the KKK was at the forefront of unsolved Black deaths during the 1950s and 1960s, according to the Southern Poverty Law Center.

In Irma's incident, there were so many dangers, including the fire being set and the possibility of it getting out of control, the gun her father held misfiring, and the unpredictable racial animus of vitriolic White racists. And in light of these perils, there was no consideration of Irma and her sibling's age because it didn't matter. But this was not Mrs. Lewis's only experience as a youth, as she admits, "Everything that happened to me coming up back then, I think about it. I can recall it just like it was yesterday." She talked about an incident where some White people attempted to poison the entire family and other Black families by contaminating the well water with a dead cat's carcass, as, at that time, the well was the only water resource.

Irma went on to discuss another experience in her youth, where, similar to the incident of the Klan burning a cross in her yard, she was an observer yet still felt the trauma of being Black. She tells the story as follows:

> My oldest brother, Elijah Wasp Jr., had been off to the Korean War … And he was back home. And so mama and daddy and him, they went up to the store. Now, at this store, my [older] brother Nook worked at the store for the Klumps. It was a grocery store … And so that Sunday morning, they went to the grocery store, and this old man, Joe Klump, he would kick all the Black men in the booty and would just laugh. And so this particular Sunday, when Mama and Daddy and Bubba [Elijah Jr.] was in there, he kicked Bubba. And when he kicked Bubba, Bubba turned around and knocked him with his fist. He went one way, and the glasses went the other way. And Momma and Dad, I thought they were going to die because he had hit a White man. And that was something you didn't do back in the day. And they came home, and I had an uncle named Uncle Theodore, and he kept money, and daddy went to him and asked him to lend him some money so he could send Bubba away because they were saying, "Well, the White folks going to come and get him and ain't nothing that [we] could do." They wouldn't be able to protect Bubba … I looked at my mama. I know I was every bit of twelve [years old]. And I looked at my poor mama, and it looked like to me my mama's hair turned

> grey because that was just how worried she was. And Daddy didn't do nothing, but just walk up and down the floor saying, "Lord, I can't do nothing! Ain't nothing I could do." They were waiting for the police to come, and my mama was so upset until her cycle came back on her. That's how scared they was. And I was sitting on the floor in the corner just looking as a little girl. I was just sitting there looking at them, and all they were saying, "Lord, ain't nothing we could do."

Irma's account ends with her brother being arrested. She and her family believe the only reason he was not killed is because the police transported him to Fairhope, Alabama, rather than Bay Minette, Alabama. In Fairhope, perhaps through some means unknown to twelve-year-old Irma, her brother was not seen as the aggressor in the incident and was eventually released.

Irma's account is traumatizing to hear; therefore, one could imagine how traumatizing it was to experience. But in her recounting of this particular racial incident, she reveals another way in which racial trauma robs Black youth. It robs them of full parents — parents are reduced to survivalists instead of the multifaceted procreators that embody a variety of parent-to-child needs. Mrs. Lewis's childhood was filled with incidents like this, where in each incident, her father and mother acted as only protectors of her and her siblings. So much so that it appears that protection was their primary role, if not the sole role. This in no way discounts the efforts of Stella and Elijah Wasp, Irma's parents, rather it indicts a racial system. It shows how the experiences of being Black, which seeks to terminate Black youth, change the entire parenting style of Black parents. The constant trauma of White systems terminating the lives of Black youth places Black parenting in a mode of perpetual trauma. It is a trauma that is a paradox because as Black parents try to protect their children, yet they simultaneously know there is little they can do to protect them from an entire system that seeks their termination. When Elijah Wasp, Irma's father, paced back and forth, mumbling to the Lord because there was nothing he could do, despite the level of courage or care he could muster, he was in real time demonstrating how being Black robs Black youth of full aspects of the parents. James Baldwin (as cited by Eddie Glaude Jr., 2020) states it like this.

> You watch your children growing up and no matter what you do, no matter what you do, you are powerless, you are really powerless, against the force of the world that is out to tell you that your child has no right to be alive … every Negro mother and father has had to face that child and try to create in that child some way of surviving this particular world, some way to make the child who will be despised not despise himself. (105)

At some point, perhaps when Black children reach adulthood, referencing those the system does not kill, one would surmise that they reclaim their parents. That if being Black reduces their parent's primary goal to ensure the survival of their children, once that is achieved (in the sense of Black children reaching adulthood), they would reclaim the other aspects of their parents. However, once a Black child is robbed of the multifaceted nature of parenting, they never reclaim it because they never stop being racialized as Black. Their parents are perpetually placing themselves as a buffer between their children and a racist system, even once they reach adulthood. The voluntary admissions of Irma show this in a way that is connected to one of the greatest tragedies of racial history, the Rosewood Massacre.

> After I was grown and had my family, and I would go over and stay with her. And every time I'd go over there, she'd sit down and she'd tell me about Rosewood, Florida. And I didn't know. I said to myself, "Why mama, keep telling me this here mess?" That's what I said, "Why she keep telling me this mess over and over and over?" Every time I come over there, she'd tell me how they had went down to Florida, down there to work. Her, her brother Willie (he was the baby boy), and her brother Ike. They had went down there to work, she say. And she said them White people came in there riding them horses and killing Black people and say they were running. Said they stayed in ditches, and they hid ... And mama say they didn't stop running. Say they ran and they ran and they hid. They hid in ditches. And say when they got, when they saw Jay, Florida, saw the sign that says, Jay, Florida say that's when they stopped running. Say because then all they had to do was cross the line and go on over into Escambia County into Pollard, Alabama, where they [eventually] lived.

Irma's mother, Stella, was born on April 26, 1910, and was twelve years old when she and her brothers managed to survive the Rosewood Massacre that happened in January of 1923. In that fact alone, we see how being racialized as Black attempted to rob Stella of her life. She was only twelve years old when White terror sought to kill her. But, also, we see how Stella telling this horrifying tale to her daughter was a form of protectionism. Perhaps she was attempting to protect her from ever venturing into the physical location of Rosewood, or perhaps, and more likely, she was instilling a sense of caution in her daughter Irma that White systems seek to extinguish Black lives and now that she herself was a mother, she would have to understand this to protect her own family. It was Stella's version of "The Talk" — the intentional family narrative in Black households that mixes truthful storytelling with caution in order to prepare Black members of the family for existing in a world that seeks their destruction (Solis, 2021).

Conclusion

When W. E. B. Du Bois (1903) said, "The problem of the Twentieth Century is the problem of the color line," he was wrong or rather shortsighted. Color, or race, is not the problem of the twentieth century. It is the problem of America because before and after the 1900s, one clear aspect of race is apparent even though ignored — society has deemed Black life dispensable. Sebastian Weier says Black people "are invisible in the discourse of a civil society that has historically been structured around the fact that Blacks were neither citizens nor human" (420). This invisible and indispensable characterization of Black people is never more pronounced than when they are youths because, at a stage of life where they are most vulnerable, society seeks not to preserve their humanity but to destroy them. George Stinney, Emmett Till, Trayvon Martin, Tamir Rice, and Antwon Rose are all examples of a system that terminates young Black lives, but such tragedies are normalized to the point where there is little to no repercussion for such actions.

Even if Black youth manage to see adulthood, their childhood was still likely robbed of natural human dignity, often being characterized as unintellectual, immoral, and deviant. Often facing more arduous life paths, not because of their actions, but because of the negative characterizations imposed on them. Black childhoods are often not healthy, but the abnormal nature by which there is a perpetual sense of survivalism has been normalized.

The life of Mrs. Irma Lewis is a testament to how being racialized as Black, separate from any actions of her own, robs Black youth. Like George Stinney, being Black had assigned a death sentence to Stella, Irma's mother, that she, fortunately, managed to escape. That cycle continued with Irma when the Klan burned a cross in the front yard, attempting to incite a reaction by which they would feel justified in their desire to destroy the Wasp Family, including an innocent Irma who was then a child. Several traumatic incidents made the survival of Irma and her siblings the priority for her parents. Even when Irma was a fully grown adult, Stella continued to tell her the traumatic story of her survival escaping Rosewood because sharing survival stories had become her method of parenting, even though Irma was then grown and had a family of her own. Her mother's desire to protect her didn't end, yet the only thing she could give as an aging woman with a lifetime of racial trauma was the survival stories.

Thus, when W. E. B. Du Bois wrote *The Souls of Black Folk* in 1903, and evoked that race was the issue of the twentieth century, perhaps he was hopeful that some reckoning would happen and that it would not perpetually be a problem of our society. But by 1920, perhaps after seeing more of the nature of race, he made a statement that is true in perpetuity — "There is no place for Black Children in this world" (Du Bois, 1920, 202).

Chapter 6

"Do You Know That Black 'Hard Work' Is Not the Answer?"

> I want every child in America to know that you are a part of the most exciting and incredible adventure in human history. No matter where your family comes from, no matter your background in America, anyone can rise with hard work, devotion, and drive.
>
> — Donald Trump, 2020

This quote is from President Trump's remarks at the 2020 Republican National Convention, and it conveys what almost every politician in modern history has articulated — a notion that individual hard work overcomes any institutional or structural disadvantage one may face. But should we unquestioningly accept this narrative? Almost every elected official has voiced some iteration of the "hard work" narrative, despite political party or ideology. As a matter of fact, sixteen years before former President Trump's narration, rising political star of the Democratic Party and then-Senator Barack Obama stated similar words when discussing his father at the Democratic National Convention. Two ideological opposing parties with two politicians who are as opposite as possible, evoking the same notion that hard work trumps all incumbrances. This is likely because it is an accepted truth for the larger American society, or better yet, it was an accepted truth present in the founding of American society and has never been relinquished.

The men deemed the Founding Fathers accepted notions of philosophy from the European continent — philosophies about life created in an all-White vacuum. I make this assertion because many of the "American values" are taken from the philosophies of men like John Locke and Thomas Hobbes, who had no understanding of a multiracial society. For example, Thomas Hobbes writes, sometimes incoherently, about the nature of humankind in his work *Leviathan*. Hobbes affirmed that all persons are born equal, a concept that appears in the Declaration of Independence. However, Hobbes's understanding of inherent human sameness at birth was that there was no inequality in the natural state of man, that "the difference between man and man is not so considerable as that one man can claim to himself any benefit" (Hobbes, 1651, 29). Simply put, as long as humans apply natural laws to societies, inequality cannot exist. The early architects of the United States embraced this flawed understanding of equality. White, literate, wealthy men, likely delusional about their own privilege and believing that America was unique and superior to any organized attempt at the nation-state, engrained this notion into American society while owning other men (that is, slaves), especially since they thought the American society did not have the socioeconomic hierarchies of Europe.

These men, including Benjamin Franklin, embraced this notion of hard work and being self-made, even believing their good fortune was a result of their work ethic. According to Heike Paul's book, *The Myths That Made America*, Benjamin Franklin confused good fortune with hard work. This is because Franklin shifted his career from the manual labor of printing and owning a print shop to being a statesman and politician, a shift he made just as economic fortunes shifted away from craftsmen (372–73). Basically, he was lucky but framed it as hard work. American culture and society have adopted this myth of hard work and being self-made, partially rooted in Hobbes's warped view of equality. But this notion does not consider the discriminatory nature of race, which, through laws, practices, and traditions, places people in unequal places at birth, an unequal place that one cannot work their way out of.

According to the peer-reviewed research of Christopher DeSante, Americans have held on to the notion that people are responsible for their own condition. DeSante (2013) notes that particularly regarding poverty, US citizens believe that a person endures poverty because of their own individual actions. He goes as far as to say that this unwavering commitment to rugged individualism and hard work is uniquely American and may be why some are so against redistributive policies and social welfare programs. This notion is supported statistically by data from the Pew Research Center, which has been asking survey questions on life determination and hard work since 2003, admittedly not consistently or systematically. In 2003, a report from Pew titled *The 2004 Political Landscape* showed that 67 percent of Americans disagreed with the notion that success in life is determined by outside forces, meaning that they believe in individual effort as the determination of success, and 68 percent believed that hard work guaranteed success. In 2007, Russell Heimlich, a Pew Reporter, reported that 62 percent still believed in individualism and that success was not determined by outside forces. And in the 2019 Pew Report, *In a Politically Polarized Era*, 60 percent of Americans believed that "most people can get ahead if they're willing to work hard."

Americans have held on to the notion of hard work since before the Constitution was ratified. This, unfortunately, is often applied without consideration of the institutional and structural disadvantages one faces when they are not White. As a result, many White Americans ignorantly believe that the statistics showing Black Americans lagging in income or wealth are not a result of the discriminatory nature of race but because Black Americans have not worked as hard as White Americans. We saw in the narrative of Jacqueline Simmons presented in an earlier chapter that the very system of capitalism attempts to keep Black people from working, thereby limiting their income and wealth. Still. perhaps no other data source clearly shows this better than the American National Election Study (ANES) — a research collaboration of Duke University, the University of Michigan, the University of Texas at Austin, and Stanford University, with funding from the National Science Foundation. In every year of collected data since 1986, the majority of Americans felt that Black citizens "are not trying hard enough" and "would be just as well off as Whites" if they worked harder, the year 2020 being the only exception.

Data from multiple trusted sources clearly demonstrate that the "hard work" philosophy is strong and widely accepted in the United States. However, it is also highly racialized, as revealed in the data from the ANES evidence that a majority of Americans feel that Black people would be in a better societal position if they worked as hard as Whites. But is this true? Would Black people be in a better societal position if they worked as hard as White people? I think that question ignorantly presumes that Black people do not work as hard as White people and confers a stereotype of laziness on them, but let's explore it nonetheless.

Figure 6.1. Black citizens "are not trying hard enough" and "would be just as well off as Whites" if they worked harder, 1986–2020. *Source*: The American National Election Study Time Series Cumulative Data File. Public domain.

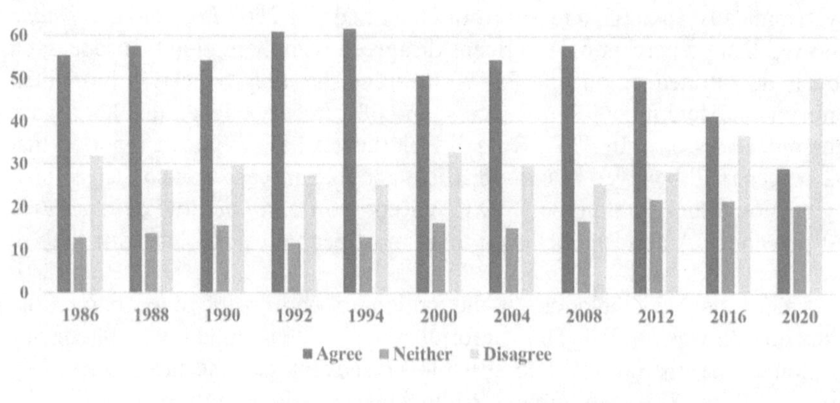

Black Hard Work Is Not the Answer

In 2015, Darrick Hamilton, William Darity Jr., Anne Price, Vishnu Sridharan, and Rebecca Tippett answered this question with a resounding "no." In a project funded by Duke University's Research Network on Racial and Ethnic Inequality, this team analyzed wealth in America to show that for Black families, "working hard is not associated with the same levels of wealth amassed among Whites" (3). Individual effort does not lead to economic success. This is true for two reasons. First, and contrary to the public opinion data presented earlier, where Americans mostly feel that outside factors have no impact, outside factors impact racial groups differently. In the Hamilton et al. (2015) study, it is found that the Great Recession of 2005 to 2009 had drastically different impacts on families — White families saw a 16 percent depletion in wealth, whereas Black families saw a 53 percent depletion in wealth. Black families are likely to burn through more wealth in times such as economic downturns because Black employees, particularly Black men, are fired first, according to the research of Kenneth Couch and Robert Fairlie (2010). This means that aside from their individual work effort or expertise in their careers, Black employees are seen as dispensable. It seems that Mrs. Simmon's notion is correct — American capitalism treats its workforce differently based on race because a hardworking Black employee is terminated first during economic hardships before a White employee with lesser expertise.

Second, and to the credit of the Hamilton et al. (2015) study, when one actually assesses individual factors that are believed to impact wealth, including labor, education, and family creation, it is discovered that wealth cannot be explained by these individual factors alone. One may be provoked to ask how this study can counter all of the latest data that shows education increases wealth. The US Federal Reserve is resolute in affirming that those with higher levels of education experience higher rates of financial well-being. This Hamilton et al. study does not contradict the Federal Reserve. It does, however, place such affirmations into a racial perspective — education does not determine wealth accumulation for Black Americans in the same way as it does for White Americans. As a matter of fact, White families where the head of household started college but did not obtain a college degree have more wealth than Black families with graduate degrees. If one were to quantify years of educational attainment, this means that even if a Black person worked six years (four years for a bachelor's degree and two more for a master's degree), that work would not amount to the wealth of a White person who has only two years (some college). The Black person worked longer and undoubtedly harder, yet does not have the wealth outcome of a White person whose work effort was only one-third that of the Black person.

If the hard work narrative is not true, why do so many Americans believe it, particularly in regard to Black Americans? Why do White people infer that Black people do not work as hard as they do? In other words, why do White people generally see Black people as lazy? The answer is that imposing a lazy narrative on Black people — the racial group that has arguably worked the hardest enduring centuries of oppressive labor under the systems of slavery and sharecropping — is that the narrative is linked to a particular type of interpersonal racism, most commonly known by the name "racial resentment."

Racial resentment may also be referred to as "symbolic racism," as coined by Cardell Jacobson (1985) decades ago. And according to the characterization of racial resentment by David Sears (1988), two things clearly manifest from individuals positioned in this prejudice. Sears says that racial resentment or symbolic racism "blended some anti-Black feeling with the finest and proudest of traditional American values, particularly individualism" (Sears, 1988, 54). First, individuals who lean into this narrative of Black laziness or the need for Black Americans to work harder embrace anti-Black sentiment, whether conscious or unconscious. These sentiments can range from false notions that Black remedial programs give Black people unfair advantages to acceptance of stereotypes and seeing microaggressions as harmless. Second, those same persons cleave proudly to American traditional ideals, even if those ideals are ahistorical, such as notions of self-realized individualism.

Social scientists sought ways to assess an individual's level of racial resentment. It was originally measured by testing attitudes along three measures: (1) "Blacks were too demanding," inputted to measure antagonism toward Blacks; (2) "resentment that governmental prescriptive measures towards Blacks," inputted to measure the perception that Blacks were receiving unwarranted social and political advantages; and (3) the denial of continued discrimination (Sear, 1988). Social scientists added a fourth measure later that is most relevant to this study and one that referenced early with the data presented from the ANES — Black Americans disadvantage stemming from their unwillingness to work hard (Sears, et al., 1997).

In less academic jargon, racial resentment explains White people's notion that Black people should work harder because it allows them to feel exonerated from critiques of an unfair racial system while holding on to values that they believe are uniquely American. It allows them to maintain a moral self-view while giving cover for the latent, and sometimes not so latent, anti-Black attitudes. Holding on to the harder work narrative makes White people feel good about themselves under the delusion that wealth and other accumulations were always achieved through self-realization, which in turn serves as proof from them regarding their already held beliefs about Black people being lazy.

However, let's say the reader still believes that the evidence presented is fabricated or slanted. That reader may still assume that if Black people worked hard and accumulated wealth, they would be as well off as their White peers, neighbors, and colleagues — that hard work and self-realization are what Black people should strive for to improve their condition. Perhaps if we return to the interviews of transgenerational Black Americans, we can come to a consensus; after all, who better to discuss the real lived experiences of being racialized as Black better than those who have a lifetime to reference?

Introducing Betsy L. McCarroll Johnson (born in Pocahontas, Arkansas, on May 18, 1948)

Betsy Johnson, similar to several other interviewees, talked about her earliest experience when her race made it apparent to her that she would face different life experiences, and this realization came when she was still a child. She recalled how, at the age of nine, she still remembered sitting in segregated theaters on the weekends. She described how the theater had "maybe ten or twelve seats in the corner" where non-White persons sat. Black patrons would be escorted upstairs to this section to ensure compliance with segregation. Even though they had paid for their tickets like White patrons, they were secluded in that segregated section and prohibited from even going to the concession stand to get refreshments. This experience may not surprise anyone, as a segregated movie theater in the South in 1957 was the norm. However, Betsy came from a hard-working family that had managed to accumulate some symbols of financial stability, even more so than some White families in the small town of Pocahontas, Arkansas. During the course of the interview, she voluntarily began to talk about the community, saying there was "lots of money there," and when asked if any Black families had money, she affirmed the hard work of her father and her family's assets, saying: "Well, my family owned two or three hundred acres. My dad raised cattle—pigs and hogs … Yes, we had money … We later had an indoor toilet. The first ones [Black or White] to have an indoor toilet. So most of the Whites in that town thought my dad had lots of money … the name "McCarroll," it meant something then, and it means something now [in Pocahontas]."

Still, the wealth and name recognition would not, dare I say could not, exempt Betsy and her family from the humiliation of discriminatory treatment simply because they were Black. This is the recognition failure of most White people. As data demonstrated, most White people believe that hard work would level the playing field without ever assessing the illogical nature of that position. As already discussed in chapter 4, the disadvantageous nature of race is sustained and cultivated by institutions — organizations with traditions, norms, policies, and cultures. The institutions are steeped in decades and sometimes centuries of discrimination; they have perfected it, and yet one Black person's dedication and resolve is supposed to undo all that after only a few years of disciplined work. This is not logical. As a matter of fact, it is insulting to Black people to think that we would buy such an argument — an argument that refuses to advocate for equitable rules but informs Black people to outwork the rules to be on par with persons who benefit from privilege. There was no measure of hard work Betsy's family could perform to overcome the racial system that caused insulting inconvenience to her family just so Betsy could get an education. She talked about it as follows:

> So we had to ride a bus fifty-five miles one way to school, to the nearest Black school, which is in Newport, Arkansas.… We

Figure 6.2. Betsy L. McCarroll Johnson, interviewed on November 12, 2023. *Source*: Provided by the author. Used with permission.

were driven every day to WF Branch High School. The closest, well, it wasn't exactly the closest Black school, but by the Board of Education Standards, the next school, which was [in] Tuckerman, Arkansas, we would be unable to get the kind of education that they thought we should have after driving fifty-five miles one way.... We were on a little fifteen-passenger bus. The speed limit was fifty-five, and if I'm correct, we got up about five o'clock every morning. Had to be [at] the bus stop at six. The bus made seven or eight stops around the community to pick up all the Black children. Then, we drove fifty-five miles to school; had to be at school, I think it started at 7:45 a.m. every day.... I was 13. And, you know, we would drive up and down and drive up and down by the highway. And in some of those cities, some of those towns we went through every morning, there was either a policeman or a state trooper.... So that would keep us all safe. You have to understand that on [the road from] Pocahontas all the way to Newport, there were no other Blacks until we got to about ten miles from Newport. Then there were

> Blacks. We went through all these towns when there were absolutely no Blacks.

How did the hard work of Betsy's family keep her from having to ride fifty-five miles to school six years after the *Brown v. Board of Education* ruling that outlawed segregation in schools? How did her father's measures of success negate the need for state troopers to protect teenagers going to school? Even with some luxuries of the time, like an indoor toilet, did all of that hard work prevent her and the Black families of the community from being relegated to the immense inconveniences?

Still, the skeptic is likely thinking, how do the unfortunate experiences of a Black girl in the South during the height of the Civil Rights Movement translate into a counter for hard work presently? To properly answer this question, two facts must be established. First, the reader should know that experiences shape identity. The happenings of life shape who a person becomes on a conscience level. Nancy Whittier says that when a person's personal experiences "are a product of societal oppression," it changes how the individual is connected to society (Whittier, 2017, 376). The reoccurring racial experiences common to Black people inform us who we are and how we should navigate the world. For Betsy, the recurring experience of having to drive fifty-five miles to school when there was a school less than a mile from her residence shaped her each time the experience happened. She became rigid and tense as she talked about how the experience shaped her — each day, the Black students of Pocahontas, Arkansas, had eight different grade levels in one classroom after a restless fifty-five-mile drive with minimal resources. That would not be an ideal educational environment under any circumstances, and as a result Mrs. Johnson said, "I think because of that, there were many of us, we missed out on so many opportunities. Educational-wise, we went to school in a one-room school; eight grades. We were behind …"

Betsy volunteered another life experience when she could finally attend an integrated school. Her own words clearly show that racism lingers or continues, but also show how it shapes a person's identity.

> My senior year, they integrated schools, and we went to the high school that was less than a mile from my house … It was the saddest day of my life because I had to leave all my Black friends … When we integrated Pocahontas High, there was nobody out there saying, "Oh, we don't want you here" or calling you the *n*-word. They ignored us as though we were not there. And to me, that was worse!

All of the earlier life experiences had conditioned her to expect some negative action from society — a literal expectation to be mistreated. But in her opinion, to be ignored was worse because it was a failure even to acknowledge her existence. Being ignored stayed with Betsy for years. It shaped her, and when she had an opportunity to return back to Pocahontas for a high school reunion, where she voiced how that had shaped her to the same individuals who had ignored her years prior. "We had a couple of teachers that I didn't forget them. I was able to explain to them how they made us feel when I went back to a reunion once upon a time. And he'd just sit there and he just cried because I could not understand how you can just be ignored. We've never been ignored. They called you something. They said something. That was the worst part. Those were the teachers."

Second, and to the question of unfortunate experiences during the Jim Crow era, the reader must be fully conscious that, so far, we have only heard a few traumatizing incidents from a lifetime of racial trauma and mistreatment. The incidents of racial mistreatment and racism against Black Americans simply because they are racialized as Black are not isolated occurrences. They are not exceptions to the rule; they are the rule! These are the common everyday lived experiences, which, if every incident were transcribed, would exceed any readable manuscript. And even though most of the more traumatic experiences seemed to be from a different time, there are no fewer examples from which Black Americans can pull today. Betsy affirmed this in the interview in her own way, "Even though it was way back then, now that I'm older, it has not stopped. It is a continuation!" Though the forms of racism may have changed, the humiliation, the inconveniences, and the dehumanization remain, and that's why Mrs. Johnson affirms, "it has not stopped." Such is the reality of the Black existence, and it is the limitation of text space that only allows for the detailing of a few incidents.

With all the hard work Betsy's father and grandfather had done, none of it mattered racially because they were still Black. Betsy and her family were not exempt from racism because hard work has no nullifying power over race. Toward the end of her interview, Betsy hammered home the notion that hard work does nothing to alleviate the ills of racism and the mistreatment of a racialized system.

> We should not have to be going through the same things that we're going through now. Just because you're Black, you are judged by the way you look, whether you got braids, dreads, how you dress, [or] what religion you are. They don't even get to how much brains you have or the language you speak. They don't even know how intelligent you are. They just judge you by the way you look. That has not changed. I'm sorry to say it's not changed.

Betsy's narration affirms the definition of Black offered in this book, as she clearly articulates that having biological features opposite those of European descent have predetermined narratives, even false narratives created about them by people who are actively ignorant of their humanity. These people do nothing to learn of that humanity, and no matter the inherent giftedness or the hard work put in by Black people, it is irrelevant as society would not take the time to learn of it anyway.

Conclusion

Since before the inception of this country, European society has leaned into a narrative of hard work. And even when their circumstances could be classified as luck or favor, they still turned to a hard-work narrative, perhaps to appease their own guilt for having privilege. The majority of Americans throughout the country have embraced this notion of hard work. It has been embraced with such unquestionable verity that the majority of White people believe that Black people would be as well off as White people if they just worked harder. A narrative that is laughable, as it assumes Black people don't work hard, but also ignores the residual effects of the 246 years of slavery (1619–1865), another 100 years of Jim Crow (1865–1964), and decades of racially targeted mass incarceration. Even if Black hard work was the answer, how does one outwork 400 years of dehumanization?

The answer is that you cannot. Black hard work is not the answer, and such a narrative is simply a furtherance of racial resentment rooted in stereotypes that Black people are lazy. It is a stereotype that allows the racial system to feel vindicated in how it has treated its Black citizens, well, as long as it has acknowledged them as citizens. But we see from the impassioned interview of Mrs. Betsy Johnson that when Black families work hard and achieve some small symbols of success, that does not stop them from being Black, and it does not exempt them from the racial mistreatment the system assigned to those racialized as Black. I have no other way to articulate it other than this: If society deems you derogatorily as a "nigger" and you work hard, then you don't stop being a "nigger." You're just a "hard-working nigger!"

Chapter 7

"Do You Know It's Not Black People's Responsibility to Fix This?"

"Black and Brown People Have Been Protesting for Centuries. It's White People Who Are Responsible for What Happens Next." This was the headline of a June 2020 article published by *Time* magazine during what has been coined the "racial awakening." One can critique whether the racial awakening was an actual shift in race relations in the US or if it was all performative in response to the triggering video footage of violence against Black people in 2020. This is particularly worthy of consideration in light of recent attacks on diversity, equity, and inclusion (DEI). However, the sentiment of the *Time* article is accurate and was so years, dare I say decades, before the worldwide protest of 2020 — the system of race was created by White people, and the disparities and disadvantages innate to the system cannot be remedied if White people make the matter of race a *Black problem*

One of the not-so-subtle messages of this book is that White people created race as a social arrangement to grant and sustain White benefits; and as chapter 1 outlines, the attempt of White people to exonerate themselves of racism by claiming proximity to the very Black people they placed and keep in a racial category of oppression is illegitimate and downright nonsensical. However, the continued and frequent claim of Black proximity proves the need to be reeducated on the subject of race. There is an unhumorous irony that the privilege White societal architects gave themselves when they made racial categories would cause White people to be the most ignorant on the subject of race.

I began this reeducation in chapter 2 by showing that even the legal definition of the Black racial group conveys a misunderstanding of race, and through the case of Sarah Rector, showed that there are factors beyond skin color in the conceptualization of race. Building from the case and the response of the White legal system, I provided the three-part definition of the Black racial group that consistently validated itself across every historical label of Black people. Indeed, Black people are those in the racial group whose visual distinctions are most opposite those of European origin for whom White active ignorance determines a sociopolitical identity rooted in disadvantage based on prevailing false narratives.

In chapters 3, 4, 5, and 6, I address differing aspects of race sociology that merit reeducation, whether prompted by White stereotypes, myths, or dissonance. In each chapter, I meticulously walk the reader through the misperception and follow up with an accurate understanding by centering research, data, and the real lived experiences of transgenerational Black Americans — experiences common to the average Black American. In chapter 3, I reeducate regarding the stereotype that Black people are inherently angry by correcting the narrative that Black people exist in systems of racial trauma, using Eve Carlson's explanation of trauma. In that chapter, I introduced William Catching and Harriet Waters who shared lived experiences of racial trauma absent the hostilities of anger, even though their life experiences would justify anger.

In chapter 4, I reeducated on the misperception that oppressive experiences of Black people are uniquely interpersonal. I affirmed the assertions of author and activist James Baldwin in that institutions, not just individuals, are culpable in sustaining the disadvantageous outcomes experienced by Black people. Then using the police as an institutional case study, I substantiate Baldwin's claim. Last, in that chapter, the reader is introduced to Jacqueline Simmons, whose life experiences show how US institutions can, and often do, harm Black people while benefiting White people.

In chapters 5 and 6, I exposed two of the dehumanizing ways the system of race determines the treatment of Black people. In chapter 5, I showed how race robs Black youth of healthy childhoods, as Black youth are rarely seen as the innocent carefree adolescents that White youth are. Being racialized as Black attempts to rob Black youth of life, and if survival is achieved, it attempts to rob their inherent humanity through unfounded presumptions of being immoral or unintellectual. I situate these claims with the life narrative of Irma Lewis, whose real lived childhood experiences paint a damning portrait of race. In chapter 6, I furthered my reeducation in anticipation of counterarguments that the book's detailing of racial inequities is because Black people have not worked as hard as White people. Using national data and the narratives of Betsy Johnson, I unapologetically affirm that there is no level of individual work to be done that can alleviate system-assigned experiences.

Who's Going to Fix This?

In the US, racialization is used to keep those who fit a category of White/European ancestry privileged and others with visible features that did not fit Eurocentric standards disadvantaged. So, if White power structures, run by White people, created this discriminatory categorization, why is it that whenever the system becomes fragile because of those realities, such as in 2020, White people ask minorities, particularly Black people, to do the labor of correction? Two years after the protests of 2020, Pew Research released a report, *Black Americans Have a Clear Vision for Reducing Racism but Little Hope It Will Happen*. While it may have been the intent of the report composers to center Black thought in the conversation of racial equity, the report, as written, infers that the skepticism in achieving racial equity can be overcome when Black people develop the strategies. And though White people should listen to

Black people (to be discussed momentarily), placing the responsibility of strategy finding on Black people is just another way of shifting responsibility from where it belongs — those who created the discriminatory systems, to begin with. The reality of expecting Black people to "pull themselves up by their own bootstraps" in a way that alleviates White people and institutions of any real remedial work is not a new notion. It is as old as reconstruction; just ask Booker T. Washington.

There is a reluctance by White society to do the hard work to achieve racial equity, perhaps because some are conscious of their privilege and don't want to lose it. Or perhaps it is because being White allows them the privilege to know nothing of anyone else, and fixing the system would require learning how the perfect *American experiment* is far from perfect. Dr. King was correct when he affirmed, "It is an aspect of their sense of superiority that the White people of America believe they have so little to learn" (King, 1967). However, if the White reader has made it this far in this reeducation, then they can no longer claim complete ignorance. The reader at least has foundational knowledge about the creation of race, how the system assigns treatment to Black people historically, and present-day narratives and data that prove that there has been insufficient system-correction. And with this foundational knowledge, I would presume that the reader wants to know: "What should I do with this knowledge?" That reader, who is now more relatively conscious of the manifestations of a racialized society than his peers, should be encouraged to act in a way that limits, if not outright prevents, the disadvantageous essence of race. I pose this thought because Savala Nolan, author of the referenced *Time* article, says that White people "generally don't know what to do with new knowledge if and when they have an aha moment, except feel guilty and let that guilt push them deeper into silence" (Nolan, 2020, para. 6).

The guilt one may feel is an acceptable emotion, as it is likely a realization that you have performed some action or failed to perform an action that has, at a minimum, sustained the racial hierarchy. But the retreat into silence and inaction is unacceptable! Allowing guilt to coerce silence and inaction is a manifestation of White fragility. I make this claim because retreat, even inwardly, is a defensive reaction, and defensiveness is the prime indicator of fragility, as explained by Robin DiAngelo. DiAngelo says that White fragility is "a state in which even a minimum amount of racial stress becomes intolerable, triggering a range of defensive moves" (2011, 54). When guilt triggers defensiveness, it allows those with privilege to engage in words and actions that defend their own perceived morality rather than the validity of the claim being presented.

Still, let's take the position that the data, research, and life narratives presented in this book were accurate. So, rather than defensiveness prompted by guilt, there are actions that White people and institutions can pursue to collapse the racial hierarchies, and it begins with a cessation of Whiteness.

Stopping Whiteness

Terms like *Blackness* and *Whiteness* refer to the normalized culture associated with the respective racial groups. Since this book has detailed varying aspects of Blackness, one could logically ask: What is Whiteness? According to the scholarly expertise of Helena Liu (2020), Whiteness is a racial culture "defined by its position of social dominance and sustained through its ongoing practice of racial oppression" (154). Liu affirms that Whiteness, or White culture, is a framework solely concerned with maintaining positions of dominance and the avoidance of experiencing oppression, though often causing it. And Liu makes no distinction as to whether the cultural actions are conscious or unconscious. However, she says that there has to be an abolition of Whiteness. In other words, White people and institutions have to work in ways that relinquish their perceived dominance and eliminate oppression. There must be a true leveling of the playing field that covers laws, policies, traditions, unspoken norms, practices, and so on. However, I affirm that this dismantling has to follow a logical order. In order to achieve the aim of racial equity, there must be a willingness to prioritize the cessation of certain actions.

The first and likely obvious action in stopping Whiteness is for White people to stop using Black proximity as a defense of their perceived self. As this book began, an affirmation of Black proximity, such as having Black friends, is an illegitimate defense of racism and shows a fundamental misunderstanding of race because the non-Black person voicing such is only voicing their proximity to melanin. In such claims, you objectify Black people, turning them into pieces of evidence to exonerate your perceived moral self-view. As has been likely proven with the preceding chapters, the White person affirming their "Black friends" likely has little to no knowledge of the experiences racial categorization imposes on the Black person.

Beyond relinquishing the faulty defense of claiming Black friends, White people should relinquish their unearned moral self-view. White people and White institutions must stop thinking that their default setting is *good*, and they are not operating in some ways that are racist. John Dovidio and Samuel Gaertner state unapologetically that aversive racism—racism situated in a non-prejudicial view of self is what characterizes a "substantial portion of well-educated and liberal Whites in America" (315). And their morality cannot be based on a limited awareness of racism's existence. Simply because one is unaware of their institutional biases and personal racial disdains, especially because they believe themselves to apply equal treatment to all, does not mean they cannot operate in ways that racially disadvantage minorities, especially Black people. Often it is the very notion of egalitarianism that sustains racial oppression, because you give all persons involved the same without considering that the system has privileged some while oppressing others. Even an individual with no racial animus can, even by ignorance, sustain racism.

Additionally, when there are inroads made in racial progress, such as specific legislation, White people should stop claiming titles, especially absent expertise.

There is a segment of the White population that, once they become relatively conscious about some of the ways racialization is inherently oppressive, give themselves titles such as "ally" or "co-conspirator." Alicia Garza, cofounder of the Black Lives Matter Movement, discussed this on the *Politically Re-Active* podcast. She informs that most White people claiming the title of "ally" are passive onlookers who operate in minimal or performative ways. She specifically mentions a "Bay Area" printing shop that supposedly deemed themselves allies, operating in solidarity with Black Lives Matter. According to Garza, the company "printed up a whole bunch of flyers with Martin Luther King's image on them and warned Black Lives Matter to 'keep it safe'" (54:53–54:59). Though Garza prefers the title of "co-conspirator," she talks that either title is not about the appeasement of Black people, but rather is it about the organizing of White people to dismantle systems that benefit Whiteness while oppressing other races. Basically, in every aspect of life, titles are granted or bestowed, and the titles associated with racial solidarity are no different. One should not grant themselves a respective title, but once they dismantle systems of oppression, those most impacted will grant them the appropriate title.

Finally, an action that is likely going to continue but should cease is that White entities should stop playing the victim, as nothing about the system of race has ever made them the victim. Understanding and engaging with self-reflection in light of conversations about race and racism does not make one the punching bag of antiracist bullies. Your victimization is only a demonstration of your resistance to racial equity and your inability to relinquish your privilege. It is a retreat to White privilege. Helena Liu poignantly provides an example of this for White women: "A well-documented strategy of White feminine fragility is the way White women burst into tears when people of color challenge their racism. In deploying tears, White women play to the myth of White feminine innocence, preserving their self-image as moral people while deflecting attention away from the concerns of people of color … they too have a tendency to fall back on victimization" (2020, 148). If it is not the responsibility of Black people to remedy the disadvantage inherent to race, then it is obvious that the responsibility falls to White people. However, beyond things White people should stop doing, what should White people do?

What Should White People Do?

As a certified expert in diversity, equity, and inclusion, a tenured professor of identity politics, and academic dean, I want to share a framework that I developed alongside sociologist Elizabeth Stygar that I think is beneficial in White reeducation. In this framework, we pull together years of experience, education, and research to task White people with performing the hard work they believe themselves so ready to do. The framework has four actions: listen, unlearn, learn, work.

Listen to Black People

In almost every workshop on inequality or inequity I have ever facilitated, there arises the counterargument from a White person that there is no inequity, and if it does exist, it exists somewhere else but not in their respective organization. Some will admit to its existence but refute the evidence-based recommendations of Black people, even if the Black person offering recommendations has more expertise than they do, as if, for them, their Whiteness trumps expertise. I used to think that a portion of White people took these positions because there was not enough evidence presented to them, and so I would anticipate such assertions from White participants and then bombard them with every piece of data I could find. However, I soon realized that it was not the absence of data but the absence of listening. Again, it goes back to the words of Dr. King. "It is an aspect of their sense of superiority" (King, 1967).

The more my expertise was requested, the more I noticed these positions of resistance would always come after affirmations of unfairness evinced by data or after some testimonial from a Black audience member of their own racialized experiences. I remember one incident in 2019, where I facilitated an invited workshop at a Midwestern university that I titled "Being Black in the Classroom." The talk was attended by the university's chancellor, who, after my data-rich presentation and Black audience members providing their own experiences, proceeded to say how he just doesn't see it that way. That the solutions offered by myself and others were not feasible options for the classroom. It was at this point that it was confirmed that some White people simply were not listening.

White people understand that "listening can be risky, painful and discomforting, but indeed necessary for consciousness-raising to understand one's world from the point of view of those who have been harmed by it" (Liu, 2020, 151). So, they lean into their privilege and simply choose not to listen. In other words, listening requires, in an existence whereby privilege everything centers on Whiteness, that for a moment, Whiteness cannot be the center. And that is too uncomfortable of an exercise for most White people. Denying the existence of discrimination or oppression or being resistant to proven strategies is an indicator of someone unwilling to listen. As of 2025, there are more than forty-eight million people in the United States who have been racialized as Black. Almost every reputable national database, from Pew to the General Social Survey to Gallup to the American National Election Study, agrees that at least eight out of ten Black people readily admit to experiencing some form of racial discrimination. Thus, when White people refuse to listen, they are actively deafening the experiences of thirty-eight million Black people, insulting them as if millions of people are experiencing the exact same hallucination.

Unlearn Whiteness

Unlearning is the process of discarding false, incomplete, or antiquated ways of thinking. And, there is some overlap here with the "Stopping Whiteness" discussion earlier. However, and without apology, there are many accepted truths that White people should relinquish. Unlearn the comfortable systems of oppression simply because White people are not oppressed, or unlearn notions of entitlement, especially in public places. Amy Cooper unlearned this in 2020 when she was corrected by Christian Cooper, a Black birdwatcher, for not having her dog on a leash, according to a recounting of the incident by Brakkton Booker of NPR (2021). As Amy felt entitled not to follow the rules of Central Park, she then filed a false police report on Christian. Christian luckily recorded the incident. Though Amy was terminated from her job, it could be logically questioned if Christian had not recorded the incident, would her entitlement have led to a different outcome?

Unlearn stereotypes because Black people are not lazy, inherently dangerous, absent culture, loud, angry, prone to violence, or any other stereotype imposed on the group. Unlearn the Whiteness that attempts to make stereotypes true. For example, it is often presumed that Black is synonymous with poverty, and when White people try to impose this stereotype on Black people, it can become costly. Thus, when Black retired circuit court judge Pamela Hill-Veal was racially mistreated for using the first-class restroom on an American Airlines flight, even though she had purchased a first-class ticket, the flight attendant's insistence that the retired judge was not supposed to use that restroom has American Airlines facing a hefty discrimination lawsuit (Franklin, 2024). If there is a Black person in first class, they are not in the wrong seat; they just purchased a first-class ticket. And do not presume that they are either an athlete or an entertainer, which presents another thing that White people should unlearn, as Black people are highly intellectual.

Unlearn the myth that Black people are not intellectual enough to achieve success in a variety of fields. In spite of personal, institutional, and structural racism, Black people have managed success across fields. According to the Association of American Medical Colleges, there are more than forty-eight thousand Black Physicians. According to the American Bar Association, there are more than sixty-five thousand lawyers. And I, myself, became dean at an accredited HBCU, Harris-Stowe State University, before the age of forty. Black people accomplish these feats in spite of racial barriers.

And even after all of that unlearning, and you believe yourself ready to learn, still unlearn false notions of relinquishing privilege. Following the racial unrest of 2020, many White people, particularly millennials and Gen Z, made unfounded statements that they gave up their privilege in solidarity with the struggle that Black Americans face. Privilege is not a coat that one can take off and give to the less fortunate. The system grants one privilege, and without systemic change, that privilege remains. Harry Brod articulated the following:

> We need to be clear that there is no such thing as giving up one's privilege to be "outside" the system. One is always in the system. The only question is whether one is part of the system in a way that challenges or strengthens the status quo. Privilege is not something I take and which therefore have the option of not taking. It is something that society gives me, and unless I change the institutions which give it to me, they will continue to give it, and I will continue to have it, however noble and egalitarian my intentions." (Brod, 1989, 280)

Rather than falsely believing you can give up your privilege, use it in a way to access fields of inequity that discriminate against Black people and, once there, set those fields ablaze.

Learn Race in Autonomy

The first level of Bloom's Taxonomy — a matrix that classifies learning — situates the first level of as simply the acquisition of knowledge, but it is how that knowledge is acquired that makes it impactful and may progress one to higher categories of learning. White people and organizations should not rely on or burden Black people with the responsibility of their reeducation. Relying on others is passive learning, but as with any education, learning must be active or, as Liu says, White people should learn "to conduct their own reading and research and work out for themselves what would be most meaningful for them to do" (2020). White people should learn first through study — by study, I mean the legitimate investigation of the real experiences of those racialized as Black. This requires a centering of a Black experience beyond skin color. White people should realize that within their learning, they must not be obtrusive but unimportant, as this isn't about them. For example, most book clubs on diversity or race tend only to be exercises in narcissism, as they are ways of making groups of mostly White liberals feel good about learning one Black author. But serious study, or investigation, transcends reading and requires leaning into uncomfortable truths about the racial experience of Black people. Even for younger White Americans who feel they have been raised in environments of greater racial tolerance, there has to be an admission that their studies of race are often limited, as it "is often limited to a historical treatment of the traditional American racism of the Civil Rights Era" (Waren, 2011, 30).

But more than learning from study, there is a benefit in learning through experiment and experience. How much time do you think White people spend with those "Black friends" in Black environments, engaging with Black culture and traditions, listening to Black narratives and histories? Anecdotal evidence would inform us that White people are not sharing life experiences with Black people in Black spaces. Ibram Kendi (2019) writes that there is a tendency to "stigmatize entire Black neighborhoods as places of homicide and mortal violence," and this untrue and racist perspective keeps White people from Black spaces and sets a dynamic where their limited engagement with Black people is in White-controlled spaces (169). However, you can never fully learn about Black people because just as White people may be uncomfortable in Black spaces, they fail to see how White spaces are often dangerous for Black people (Liu, 2020). Scholar Megan Boler (as cited by Liu [2020]) says when we embrace that discomfort and "liv[e] at the edge of our skin," it is where we learn because we have the greatest hope of reenvisioning ourselves.

Work

External action, or work, is necessary! One cannot change the discriminatory nature of race if one only works to learn for oneself. There must be work performed that puts learning into practice and attacks the visible disparities experienced under a racialized system.

First, the work consists of holding White individuals and institutions accountable for the reluctance to change racist policies. Racist policies are any measure that either "produces or sustains racial inequity between racial groups" (Kendi, 2019, 18). This means that some policies, especially written ones, may not ever explicitly state racial mistreatment, but if they produce unbalanced outcomes with clear racial delineations, then that policy is racist. The Civil Rights Division of the US Department of Justice calls this disparate impact — any policy or practice that produces disproportionate outcomes for race, color, or nationality. When these policies are evinced, the work is to hold institutions accountable for sustaining and sometimes defending these policies. But this has to happen in White spaces! During every election season, you see White politicians go into Black churches, community centers, and communities, explaining how they are for Black advancement and the elimination of racist policies, but they rarely, if ever, go into the White school board meetings, HOA meetings, or churches and tell White people about the structures and rules that continually oppress Black people. Alicia Garza says the work consists of White people "checking" other White people, rules, and organizations — holding them accountable when the outcomes are racially unfair. For example:

- When you are meeting with mid-level managers, ask, "Why is there only one Black person in the room?"
- When the workers union drafted a statement voicing the commitment to racial equity, ask, "Why doesn't the statement have a definition of *equity*, or any concrete goals?
- When your White lifelong friend makes "that joke," tell him at that moment that it was racist and that if he insists on making people of color the punch line to his comedy, the friendship cannot continue.

Second, beyond accountability, the work requires undoing the normalization of Whiteness. In the US, White cultures are normal, such as the phrase "as American as apple pie." Yet I know of no Black family that eats apple pie at family reunions, Thanksgiving holidays, or special celebrations — those families tend to prefer sweet potato, pecan, or perhaps lemon meringue. There is a normalization of Whiteness that should be undone. You see, when a White person is a CEO, no one questions if they were a DEI hire. When a White person suggests a policy change, no one questions if this is some covert attempt to slide in affirmative action principles. When White people go viral in videos that lack decorum or even are violent, no one calls them "thugs" or "ghetto." These examples illustrate the normalization of Whiteness — where White people can move through the world with their needs readily met, and they are granted humanizing qualities, such as compassion, trust, and a presumption of innocence (Collins, 2018). There are traditions, written policies, and accepted realities that need to be undone and dismantled. This is the work!

In doing the work, Helena Liu offers caution to White people to do the work in a way that authentically exposes race as an inherently discriminatory categorization of people, as it assigns certain experiences to some and privileges others. She says White people will often inform of their work in a way that recenters Whiteness and presents themselves as good moral White people, what she terms "White innocence" (152). But the reality is that sometimes you will not feel good. You often will not feel innocence or exoneration. You may feel guilt or shame for your participation in the system. And as you become relatively conscious of the pervasive and discriminatory nature of race, you will find in doing the work that you will see instances in which you will lose social dominance, making the work more uncomfortable. In that moment, will you embrace equity for your Black friends?

References

11Alive. (2020, August 27). *Trump at RNC: Anyone Can Rise in America with Hard Work* [Video]. YouTube. https://www.youtube.com/watch?v=tTRB2mhOacI.

Allen, Q., and Metcalf, H. S. (2020). "Up to No Good: The Intersection of Race, Gender, and Fear of Black Men in Society." In T. D. Boyce and W. M. Chunnu (eds.), *Historicizing Fear: Ignorance, Vilification, and Othering*. University Press of Colorado.

American Bar Association. (2022, June 20). *ABA Survey Finds 1.3M Lawyers in the U.S.* https://www.americanbar.org/news/abanews/aba-news-archives/2022/06/aba-lawyers-survey/.

American Civil Liberties Union. (2003, February 26). *Race and the Death Penalty*. https://www.aclu.org/documents/race-and-death-penalty.

American National Election Study, Duke University, University of Michigan, and Stanford University. (1986–2020). ANES Time Series Cumulative Data File. Inter-university Consortium for Political and Social Research [distributor].

Archbold, C. A. (2012). "The History of the Police." *Policing a Text/Reader*. SAGE. https://www.sagepub.com/sites/default/files/upm-binaries/50819_ch_1.pdf.

Association of American Medical Colleges. (2021). *Report on Residents*. https://www.aamc.org/data-reports/students-residents/data/report-residents/2021/executive-summary.

Austin, D. (2020, July 10). "Anti-slavery Revolutionaries Who Practiced What They Preached." *The Hill*. https://thehill.com/changing-america/opinion/506782-anti-slavery-revolutionaries-who-practiced-what-they-preached/.

Austin, S. D. W. (2018). *The Caribbeanization of Black Politics: Race, Group Consciousness, and Political Participation in America*. State University of New York Press.

BBC. (2021, January 11). "Michelle Obama: 'I'm no Angry Black Woman.'" *British Broadcasting Network*. https://www.bbc.com/news/world-us-canada-16515834.

Behan, B. (2007, June 27). "Leonard 'Kip' Rhinelander Trial (1925)." *BlackPast*. https://www.blackpast.org/african-american-history/leonard-kip-rhinelander-trial-1925/.

Bell, L. A., Funk, M. S., Joshi, K. Y., and Valdivia, M. (2016). "Racism and White Privilege." In M. Adams, L. A. Bell, D. J. Goodman, and K. Y. Joshi (eds.), *Teaching for Diversity and Social Justice*, 3rd ed. (133–81). Routledge.

Bell, W. K., and Kondabolu, H. (Hosts). (2017, October 5). "What Did We Learn? With Alicia Garza and Wyatt Cenac." [Audio Podcast Episode]. In *Politically Re-Active*. Apple Podcast. https://podcasts.apple.com/us/podcast/what-did-we-learn-with-alicia-garza-and-wyatt-cenac/id1125018164?i=1000393102269.

Berry, D. R. (2019). "How Sally Hemings and Other Enslaved People Secured Precious Pockets of Freedom." *History*. https://www.history.com/news/slavery-negotiations-freedom-concubines-thomas-jefferson-sally-hemings.

Board of Governors of the Federal Reserve System. (2023). *Economic Well-Being of U.S. Households (SHED)*. https://www.federalreserve.gov/publications/2022-economic-well-being-of-us-households-in-2021-education.htm.

Boston Museum of African American History. (n.d.). "Black Boston: The North Slope of Beacon Hill." National Park Service/U.S. Department of Interior.

Brakkton, B. (2021, February 16). "Amy Cooper, White Woman Who Called Police on Black Bird-Watcher, Has Charge Dismissed." *NPR*. https://www.npr.org/2021/02/16/968372253/white-woman-who-called-police-on-black-man-bird-watching-has-charges-dismissed.

Brod, H. (1989). "Work Clothes and Leisure Suits: The Class Basis and Bias of the Men's Movement." In *Men's Lives* M. S. Kimmel and M. Messner (eds.). Macmillan.

Brown, S. (1933). "Negro Character as Seen by White Authors." *Journal of Negro Education* 2: 179–203.

Carson, E. A., and Kluckow, R. (2023). "Prisoners in 2022: Statistics Table." Bureau of Justice Statistics/U.S. Department of Justice. https://bjs.ojp.gov/document/p22st_sum.pdf.

Carter, R. T., and Pieterse, A. L. (2020). *Measuring the Effects of Racism: Guidelines for the Assessment and Treatment of Race-Based Traumatic Stress Injury*. Columbia University Press, ProQuest Ebook Central.

CBS News. (2012, December 2). *The Duality of Thomas Jefferson* [Video]. YouTube. https://www.youtube.com/watch?v=bzZnqXvRSLE&t=448s.

Civil Rights Division. (n.d.). "Section VII-Proving Discrimination-Disparate Impact." U.S. Department of Justice. [[ED: Comment from the author: I am not totally sure what to do here. I checked this URL and found that the link has been removed because the Department of Justice rescinded "enforcement" of disparate impact under the Trump Administration, even though the policy still exists.]] https://www.justice.gov/crt/fcs/T6Manual7#C.

CNN Editorial Research. (2024, February 14). *Trayvon Martin Shooting Fast Facts*. https://www.cnn.com/2013/06/05/us/trayvon-martin-shooting-fast-facts/index.html.

Couch, K. A., and Fairlie, R. (2010). "Last Hired, First Fired? Black-While Unemployment and the Business Cycle." *Demography* 47 (1): 227–47.

Coleman, K. (2013, Feb. 6). "Essie Mae Washington-Williams Dies, Mixed Race Child of Strom Thurmond." NPR. https://www.npr.org/sections/thetwo-way/2013/02/06/171273089/essie-mae-washington-williams-dies-mixed-race-child-of-strom-thurmond.

Collins, C. (2018). "What Is White Privilege, Really?" *Teaching Tolerance*. https://www.tolerance.org/magazine/fall-2018/what-is-white-privilege-really.

Contreras, R. (2024). "Pew: Most Black Americans Say Police, Government Plot Against Them" *Axios*. https://www.axios.com/2024/06/10/black-americans-police-government-beliefs.

Cox, K., and Edwards, K. (2022, August 30). *Black Americans Have a Clear Vision for Reducing Racism but Little Hope It Will Happen*. Pew Research Center. https://www.pewresearch.org/race-and-ethnicity/2022/08/30/black-americans-have-a-clear-vision-for-reducing-racism-but-little-hope-it-will-happen/.

Crenshaw, K. (2015). *Black Girls Matter: Pushed Out, Overpoliced and Underprotected*. https://www.law.columbia.edu/sites/default/files/2021-05/black_girls_matter_report_2.4.15.pdf.

De Castillo, L. G. (2018). "Unconscious Racial Prejudice as Psychological Resistance: A Limitation of the Implicit Bias Model." *Critical Philosophy of Race* 6 (2): 262–79.

DeSante, C. (2013). "Working Twice as Hard to Get Half as Far: Race, Work Ethic and America's Deserving Poor." *American Journal of Political Science* 57 (2): 342–56.

DiAngelo, R. (2011). "White Fragility." *International Journal of Critical Pedagogy* 3 (3): 54–70.

Diggs, I. (1976). "Du Bois and Children." *Phylon (1960–)* 37 (4): 370–99.

Douglass, F. (1852). *What to the Slave Is the Fourth of July?*

Dovidio, J. F., and Gaertner, S. L. (2000). "Aversive Racism and Selection Decisions: 1989–1999." *Psychological Science* 11 (4): 315–19.

Du Bois, W. E. B. (1903). *The Souls of Black Folk*. W. W. Norton.

Du Bois, W. E. B. (1920). *Darkwater: Voices from Within the Veil*. Dover.

Duhe, L. (2022, October 3). "Sen. Kennedy Suggests Critics of Police 'Call a Crackhead' in New Ad; Some Think Line Goes too Far." WAFB News. https://www.wafb.com/2022/10/03/sen-kennedy-suggests-critics-police-call-crackhead-new-ad-some-think-line-goes-too-far/.

Easton, H. (1837). *A Treatise on the Intellectual Character and Civil and Political Condition of the Colored People of the United States, and The Prejudice Exercised Towards Them*. Isaac Knapp.

Edwards, B. (June 12, 2018). "Missouri Waitress Fired over 'N-Word Hunting' Video Swears She Isn't Racist, Claims to Have Black Friends." *The Root*. https://www.theroot.com/missouri-waitress-fired-after-n-word-hunting-video-swea-1826765082.

Edwards, F., Lee, H., and Esposito, M. (2019). "Risk of Being Killed by Police Use of Force in the United States by Age, Race-Ethnicity, and Sex." *Proceedings of the National Academy of the Sciences* 116 (34): 16793–98.

Eligon, J. (2019, February 16). "The 'Some of My Best Friends Are Black' Defense." *New York Times*. https://www.nytimes.com/2019/02/16/sunday-review/ralph-northam-blackface-friends.html.

Ely, D. M., and Driscoll, A. K. (2023). "Infant Mortality in the United States, 2021: Data from the Period Linked Birth/Infant Death File." *National Vital Statistics Report* 72 (11): 1–18.

Franklin, J. (2024, February 25). "American Airlines Passenger Alleges Discrimination over use of First-class Restroom." NPR. https://www.npr.org/2024/04/25/1245583048/american-airlines-racial-discrimination-allegation-bathroom.

Gaynor, T. S., Kang, S. C., and Williams, B. N. (2021). "Segregated Spaces and Separated Races: The Relationship Between State-Sanctioned Violence, Place, and Black Identity." *Russell Sage Foundation Journal of the Social Sciences* 7 (1): 55–66.

Glaude, E. D., Jr. (2020). *Begin Again: James Baldwin's American and Its Urgent Lessons for Our Own*. Penguin Random House. Goff, P. A., Jackson, M. C., Di Leone, B. A. L., Culotta, C. M., and DiTomasso, N. A. (2014). "Essence of Innocence: Consequences of Dehumanizing Black Children." *Journal of Personality and Social Psychology* 106 (4): 526–45.

Hamilton, D., Darity, W., Price, A. E., Sridharan, V., and Tippett, R. (2015). *Umbrellas Don't Make It Rain: Why Studying and Working Hard Isn't Enough for Black Americans*.

Harper, S. R. (2012). "Race Without Racism: How Higher Education Researchers Minimize Racist Institutional Norms." *Review of Higher Education* 36 (1): 9–29.

Harris, V. J. (1990). "African American Children's Literature: The First One Hundred Years." *Journal of Negro Education* 59 (4): 540–55.

Heimlich, R. (2007, July 17). *Say People Determine Own Success*. https://www.pewresearch.org/short-reads/2007/07/17/say-people-determine-own-success/.

Hill, R. B. (2004). "Institutional Racism in Child Welfare." *Race and Society* 7 (1): 17–33.

Hobbes, T. ([1651] 2012). *Leviathan*. In Jeske, D. and Fumerton, R. (eds.). (2012). *Readings in Political Philosophy: Theory and Applications*. Broadview Press.

Jackson, C. (2021, August 17). "What Is Redlining?" *New York Times*. https://www.nytimes.com/2021/08/17/realestate/what-is-redlining.html.

Jacobson, C. K. (1985). "Resistance to Affirmative Action: Self-Interest or Racism?" *Journal of Conflict Resolution* 29: 306–29.

Johnson, G. B. (1939). "Patterns of Race Conflict." In Edgar T. Thompson (ed.), *Race Relations and the Race Problem: A Definition and An Analysis* (129–51). Duke University Press.

Johnson, S. R. (2022, November 16). "U.S. News–Harris Poll Survey: As America Aims for Equity, Many Believe Systemic Racism Doesn't Exist." *U.S. World News*. https://www.usnews.com/news/health-news/articles/2022-11-16/poll-many-americans-dont-believe-systemic-racism-exists.

Kaczorowski, R. J. (1987). "To Begin the Nation Anew: Congress, Citizenship, and Civil Rights After the Civil War." *American Historical Review* 92 (1): 45–68.

Kelly, C. (2019, February 7). "Virginia Governor Apologizes for "Racist and Offensive Costume in Photo Showing People in Blackface and KKK Garb." *CNN Politics*. https://www.cnn.com/2019/02/01/politics/northam-blackface-photo/index.html.

Kendi, I. X. (2019). *How to Be an Antiracist*. New York: One World.

Kennedy, R. L. 1999, "Who Can Say 'Nigger'? And Other Considerations." *Journal of Blacks in Higher Education* 26: 86–96.

King Institute, Stanford University. (n.d.). *Alabama Clergymen's Letter to Dr. Martin Luther King Jr.* https://www.samford.edu/arts-and-sciences/files/History/Statement-and-Response-King-Birmingham.pdf.

King, K. (2010). *African American Politics*. Polity Press.

King, M. L., Jr. (1967). *Where Do We Go from Here: Chaos or Community?* Harper & Row.

Kishi, R., and Jones, S. (2020). Demonstrations and Political Violence in America: New Data for Summer 2020. *The Armed Conflict Location and Event Data Project (ACLED)*. https://acleddata.com/2020/09/03/demonstrations-political-violence-in-america-new-data-for-summer-2020/.

Krutz, G. (2021). *American Government*, 3rd ed. Ebook. Rice University Press

Lepore, J. (2020). "The Invention of the Police." *New Yorker*. https://www.newyorker.com/magazine/2020/07/20/the-invention-of-the-police.

Lewis, T. E. (2017). "Repercussive Discrimination: Racial Discrimination as an Explanation of Prevalent Homophobia Among Racial Minorities." PhD diss., University of Missouri–St. Louis.

Lewis, T. E. (2019). "Black Curativeness: Understanding Black Voter Selection Through an Assessment of Racially-Charged Districts." *National Political Science Review* 20 (3): 136–48.

Lewis, T. E., and Nelson, S. J. (2021). "Insulated Blackness: The Cause for Fracture in Black Political Identity." *Politics, Groups, and Identities*. DOI: 10.1080/21565503.2021.1892783.

Lim, C. (2024, January 5). "Nikki Haley Says 'I had Black friends' in her Mea Culpa for Civil War Comments." *MSNBC*. https://www.msnbc.com/top-stories/latest/nikki-haley-remarks-civil-war-black-friends-statement-rcna132458.

Liu, H. (2020). *Redeeming Leadership: An Antiracist Feminist Intervention*. Bristol University Press.

Lloyd, C., and Washington, E. F. (Hosts). (2022, August 23). Food Shame at Work: An Oft-Overlooked Employee Experience [Audio Podcast]. In *Cultural Competence*. Gallup. https://news.gallup.com/podcast/397910/food-shame-work-oft-overlooked-employee-experience.aspx.

Losey, S. (2018, June 15). "Here's What the Air Force Is Doing About that Recruit in the Racist Video." *Air Force Times*. https://www.airforcetimes.com/news/your-air-force/2018/06/15/heres-what-the-air-force-is-doing-about-that-recruit-in-the-racist-video/.

Love, B. (2021, March 31). "NAACP Explains the 'Angry Black Person' Bias." ABC10. https://www.abc10.com/article/news/local/naacp-explains-angry-black-person-bias/103-dce57751-10bd-403e-81fd-4e7cec058671.

Malesky, K. (2014). "The Journey from 'Colored' to 'Minorities' to 'People of Color.'" National Public Radio. https://www.npr.org/sections/codeswitch/2014/03/30/295931070/the-journey-from-colored-to-minorities-to-people-of-color.

Martinez, M., and Booker, B. (2023, February 14). "Nikki Haley's Complicated Racial Dance." *Politico*. https://www.politico.com/newsletters/the-recast/2023/02/14/nikki-haley-2024-race-republican-party-00082772.

Middleton, Richard T., IV. (2008). "Institutions, Inculcation, and Black Racial Identity: Pigmentocracy vs. the Rule of Hypodescent." *Social Identities: Journal for the Study of Race, Nation, and Culture* 14 (5): 639–54.

Motro, D., Evans, J. B., Ellis, A. P. J., and Benson, L. (2022, January 31). The "Angry Black Woman" Stereotype at Work. *Harvard Business Review*. https://hbr.org/2022/01/the-angry-black-woman-stereotype-at-work.

NAACP (2024). *The Origins of Modern Day Policing*. https://naacp.org/find-resources/history-explained/origins-modern-day-policing.

National Museum of African American History and Culture. (n.d.). *Little Black Sambo*. https://nmaahc.si.edu/object/nmaahc_2007.7.382.

National Science Foundation. *American National Election Study—2016*. www.electionstudies.org.

NBC News. (2019). "Rashida Tlaib Accuses Meadows of 'Racist' Presentation at Michael Cohen Hearing." NBC News [Video]. YouTube. https://www.youtube.com/watch?v=NhNJF86aDJ4.

Nelson, S. J. (2021). *The Congressional Black Caucus: Fifty Years of Fighting for Equality*. Archway Publishing.

Nolan, S. (2020, June 1). "Black and Brown People Have Been Protesting for Centuries. It's White People Who Are Responsible for What Happens Next." *Time*. https://time.com/5846072/black-people-protesting-white-people-responsible-what-happens-next/.

Obama, B. H. (2004, July 27). Keynote Address at the 2004 Democratic National Convention. https://www.presidency.ucsb.edu/documents/keynote-address-the-2004-democratic-national-convention.

Obasogie, O. K. (2017). "Race and Science: Reconciliation as Reconciliation." In C. J. Ogletree and A. Sarat (eds.), *Racial Reconciliation and the Healing of a Nation* (49–61). New York University Press.

Oprah Winfrey Network. (2016). *Michelle Obama on the Stereotype of the "Angry Black Woman"*/Oprah Special/Oprah Winfrey Network [Video]. YouTube. https://www.youtube.com/watch?v=vBZRbQMEYUo.

Ortiz, S. E., and Zimmerman, F. J. (2012). "Race/Ethnicity and the Relationship Between Homeownership and Health." *American Journal of Public Health*. https://ajph.aphapublications.org/doi/full/10.2105/AJPH.2012.300944.

Parker, K., Horowitz, J. M., and Anderson, M. (2020, June 12). Amid Protests, Majorities Across Racial and Ethnic Groups Express Support for the Black Lives Matter Movement. *Pew Research Center*. https://www.pewresearch.org/social-trends/2020/06/12/amid-protests-majorities-across-racial-and-ethnic-groups-express-support-for-the-black-lives-matter-movement/.

Paul, H. (2014). "Expressive Individualism and the Myth of the Self-Made Man." *The Myths That American Made: An Introduction to American Studies*. Transcript Verlag.

PBS. (2013, October 10). "Interracial Relationships that Changed History." PBS. https://www.pbs.org/articles/interracial-relationships-that-changed-history/.

Pew Research Center. (2003, November 5). "Part 4: Success, Poverty and Government Responsibility." *The 2004 Political Landscape*. https://www.pewresearch.org/politics/2003/11/05/part-4-success-poverty-and-government-responsibility/.

Pew Research Center. (2016, June 27). "On View of Race and Inequality, Blacks and Whites Are Worlds Apart." *Pew Research*. https://www.pewresearch.org/social-trends/2016/06/27/on-views-of-race-and-inequality-blacks-and-whites-are-worlds-apart/.

Pew Research Center. (2019, December 17). "3. Views on the Economic System and Social Safety Net." *In a Politically Polarized Era, Sharp Divides in Both Partisan Coalitions*. https://www.pewresearch.org/politics/2019/12/17/views-of-the-economic-system-and-social-safety-net/.

Pew Research Center. (2022, January 5). *Do Americans Trust the Police?* [Video]. YouTube. https://www.youtube.com/watch?v=Jj9vD7cKUhE&list=PLZ9z-Af5ISaswq9yoHM32olz4-AITb1Dl.

Pittman, C. T. (2012). "Racial Microaggressions: The Narratives of African American Faculty at a Predominately White University." *Journal of Negro Education* 81 (1): 82–92.

Quallen, M. (2016). "Making Animals, Making Slaves: Animalization and Slavery in the Antebellum United States." Honors thesis, Georgetown University. Georgetown Repository. https://repository.digital.georgetown.edu/handle/10822/1040660.

Reichel, P. L. (1988). Southern Slave Patrols as a Transitional Police Type." *American Journal of Police* 7 (2): 51–78.

Reyes, M. V. (2020). "The Disproportional Impact of COVID-19 on African Americans." *Health and Human Rights* 22 (2): 299–307.

Sears, D. O. (1988). "Symbolic Racism." In *Eliminating Racism: Profiles in Controversy* P. A. Katz and D. A. Taylor (eds.). Springer US.

Sears, D. O., Colette V. L., Mary C., and Kosterman, R. (1997). "Is It Really Racism? The Origins of White Americans' Opposition to Race-Targeted Policies." *Public Opinion Quarterly* 61 (1): 16–56.

Siek, Stephanie. (2011). "Perceptions of Discrimination: A Black and White Story." CNN. https://www.cnn.com/2011/12/12/us/perceptions-of-discrimination-a-black-and-white-story.

SIU System (2020, September 21). *Conversations of Understanding: Race Based Trauma and Mental Health* [Video]. YouTube. https://www.youtube.com/watch?v=r3NFtIutW2Y&t=1584s.

Smith, T. W. (1992). "Changing Racial Labels: From 'Colored' to 'Negro' to 'Black' to 'African American.'" *Public Opinion Quarterly* 56 (4): 496–514.

Solis, G. (2021, March 10). "For Black Parents, 'The Talk' Binds Generations and Reflects Changes in America." *USC Today*. https://today.usc.edu/the-talk-usc-black-parents-children-racism-america/.

Southern Poverty Law Center. (2011). *Ku Klux Klan: A History of Racism and Violence*, 6th ed.

Southern Poverty Law Center. (2019). "Hate Groups Reach Record High." https://www.splcenter.org/news/2019/02/19/hate-groups-reach-record-high.

Special Issue, T. (2018). "Special Issue School-to-Prison Pipeline." *Taboo: Journal of Culture and Education* 17 (4): 1–6.

Stanford University. (n.d.). *Say Their Names: Green Library Exhibit in support of the Black Lives Matter Movement*. https://exhibits.stanford.edu/saytheirnames/feature/george-stinney.

Stanford University. (n.d.). *Say Their Names: Green Library Exhibit in support of the Black Lives Matter Movement.* https://exhibits.stanford.edu/saytheirnames/feature/antwon-rose-jr.

Statista. (2022). Number of Mass Shootings in the United States Between 1982 and November 2022, by Shooter's Race or Ethnicity. https://www.statista.com/statistics/476456/mass-shootings-in-the-us-by-shooter-s-race/.

Taibi, A. D. (1994, May). "Banking, Finance, and Community Economic Empowerment: Structural Economic Theory, Procedural Civil Rights, and Substantive Racial Justice." *Harvard Law Review* 107 (7): 1463–545.

The African-Native American Genealogy Blog (2010, April 24). *Remembering Sarah Rector, Creek Freedwoman.* http://african-nativeamerican.blogspot.com/2010/04/remembering-sarah-rector-creek.html.

The Dick Cavett Show. (2020, June 24). *James Baldwin and Paul Weiss's HEATED Debate on Discrimination in America. The Dick Cavett Show* [Video]. YouTube. https://www.youtube.com/watch?v=hzH5IDnLaBA.

Toland, F. (2006). "Racist Policy in American History." *African American History*. Lecture-Tuskegee University.

Treece, K. (2024). "Small Business Loan Statistics and Trends 2024." *Forbes*. https://www.forbes.com/advisor/business-loans/small-business-loan-statistics/.

University of Pittsburgh. (2024). "Exactly What's the Different European Facial Features?" *Research Data Management Committee*. https://rdmc.pitt.edu/exactly-what-the-different-european-facial-features/.

U.S. Census Bureau. (n.d.). *Race*. https://www.census.gov/quickfacts/fact/note/US/RHI625221.

U.S. Census Bureau. (2010). *Measuring Race and Ethnicity Across the Decades: 1790–2010 | Mapped to 1997 U.S. Office of Management and Budget Classification Standards*. U.S. Office of Management and Budget. https://www.census.gov/data-tools/demo/race/MREAD_1790_2010.html.

U.S. Census Bureau. (2023). *Quick Facts*. https://www.census.gov/quickfacts/fact/table/US/PST045222.

U.S. Department of Commerce — U.S. Census (2021). Additional Instructions for Respondents. https://www.census.gov/programs-surveys/decennial-census/technical-documentation/questionnaires/2020/response-guidance.html#accordion-e720ccc395-item-0df0ed5c26.

U.S. Treaty with the Creek Nation, July 19, 1866, https://www.blackpast.org/african-american-history/u-s-treaty-creek-nation-1866/.

Walton, Hanes, Robert C. Smith, and Sherri L. Wallace. (2017). *American Politics and the African American Quest for Universal Freedom*. Routledge.

Wanzo, R. (2015). "The Deadly Fight over Feelings." *Feminist Studies* 40 (1): 226–31.

Waren, W. (2011). "Using Monopoly to Introduce Concepts of Race and Ethnic Relations." *Journal of Effective Teaching* 11 (1): 28–35.

Waxman, O. (2017). "How the U.S. Got Its Police Force." *Time*. https://time.com/4779112/police-history-origins/.

Weier, S. (2014). "Consider Afro-Pessimism." *Amerikastudien/American Studies* 59 (3): 419–33.

Whittier, N. 2017. "Identity Politics, Consciousness-Raising, and Visibility Politics." In *The Oxford Handbook of U.S. Women's Social Movement Activism*, Holly J. McCammon, Verta Taylor, Jo Reger, and Rachel L. Einwohner (eds.), 376–97. Oxford University Press.

Wilkerson, I. (2020). *Caste: The Origins of Our Discontents*. Random House.

Wilkins, E. J., J. B. Whiting, M. F. Watson, J. M. Russon, and A. M. Moncrief. (2012). "Residual Effects of Slavery: What Clinicians Need to Know." *Contemporary Family Therapy* 35: 14–28.

Williams, D. T. (2023). "Racial Disparities Without Racism: Some Conceptual and Analytical Considerations." *Sociology Compass*.

Wills, Christopher. (1994). "The Skin We're In." *Discover*. https://www.discovermagazine.com/health/the-skin-were-in.

Wingfield, A. H. (2007). "The Modern Mammy and the Angry Black Man: African American Professionals' Experiences with Gendered Racism in the Workplace." *Race, Gender & Class* 14 (1/2): 196–212.

Index

www.ingramcontent.com/pod-product-compliance
Lightning Source LLC
LaVergne TN
LVHW090602070826
845179LV00020B/118